BAKE

BAKE

RORY MACDONALD

New York Paris London Milan

CONTENTS

WHERE IT ALL STARTED

When I was growing up my family always vacationed somewhere in France, never in the same region, sometimes for three to four weeks at a time. Looking back, I think it was during these trips that I really fell in love with food. Even today I can remember trying my first baguette, my first mussel, my first steak—these experiences transformed the way I looked at food. The variety of the food among the different regions of France still amazes me. My parents were both teachers whose work began early and ended late every day. They did not have time to cook elaborate meals during the week, but during the holidays and on the weekends, they would pull out all the stops.

Coming from an academic family, on our family vacations, everyone always had their head buried in a book. But, as a kid, I was unable to sit still long enough to read so the kitchen became a natural destination for me. At the time I'm sure I did not appreciate the ingredients I had access to or how lucky I was to be able to walk to a farmers' market every morning. The taste of baguettes baked fresh from a wood-burning oven and my first experience of classic recipes such as *moules et frites* and steak with green peppercorn sauce gave me a respect for food that I still have today.

From an early age I never had a doubt that cooking was what I wanted to do. Some people fall into this profession, but when I was twelve years old, I already was certain that I wanted to be a chef. At that age, I began cooking more adventurous things at home, subjecting my parents to some real disasters, which they always slowly but politely ate. At sixteen I landed my first kitchen job, in a local four-star hotel set in an old monastery; the Nutfield Priory Hotel in Surrey, England, was a beautiful historic property and its kitchen was run by an amazing executive chef named David Evans, to whom I owe so much. As soon as I finished school I was accepted into the hotel's apprenticeship program, which I completed in four years. We were taught about every department in the kitchen, and many of the dishes on the menu were designed specifically to instruct us: pig's trotters, for example—no one ever ordered them, but we had to learn how to break them down and cook them. I will always be grateful for this education; you can't really learn these things in cooking school, you need to do them under the pressure of a professional kitchen—and this was a tough kitchen. There's one particular incident from my time working there that I will never forget. One afternoon I was assigned to make sandwiches for a wedding. I was a year into my apprenticeship at that point, so I thought I knew everything and I didn't want to be stuck making sandwiches. I wanted to be filleting a whole salmon or breaking down the quail, but instead I was making hundreds of sandwiches. They didn't look good, as I didn't really care about doing them, but then Chef Evans walked past, grabbed me hard by the arm until I flinched, and asked me, "If it ain't perfect, then why bother?" Then he let go and walked away. It was like a lightning bolt had hit me: I immediately went back to the sandwiches and fixed each and every one, making sure that they were the best I could possibly make. A few hours later, when the sandwiches were leaving the kitchen, the chef looked them all over, gave me a wink, and then he kicked me straight in my shin with his pointy shoe!

It's a day I will never forget, and without David Evans's support and firm guidance, I definitely would not be writing this cookbook. The four years of my apprenticeship were some of the best in my career, and I feel very honored to have had that experience. (Incidentally I also met my now wife there, all those years ago!) Professional kitchens are tough places; many of them adhere to a survival of the fittest code, and I think that's what always drew me to them. I love the boisterousness and banter of the kitchen, and its dog-eat-dog mentality. I always try to leave a kitchen better than when I walked in, but there's always room for improvement; everyone in the kitchen is chasing a finish line but always falling just short, until another race begins. That constant need for innovation and perfection is like an addiction at times. Sure I could settle for less, but I'd never be satisfied. And Chef Evans's rhetorical question is always playing in the back of my mind: "If it ain't perfect, then why bother?"

El Bulli is still the most famous and influential restaurant in the world and it has been shut for many years now. During my apprenticeship in the early 2000s it was just beginning to get worldwide recognition, even though it had already been around for forty years. I remember reading an article in *The Observer Food Monthly* about Chef Ferran Adrià's philosophy and seeing the photographs of his food and the restaurant—after undergoing the rigors of strict French training, it was totally revolutionary to see Michelin three-star food. It didn't look perfect but it was perfect in its imperfection, which was a breath of fresh air for me. I knew I had to go to Spain.

Luckily for me, Chef Evans had a former colleague from Madrid who was (and still is) one of the most prestigious chefs in Spain; Salvador Gallego's restaurant, hotel, and school is a Michelin-starred Relais & Châteaux property, and his list of accolades is too long to include in this book. I moved to Madrid with a single bag, unable to speak Spanish, with very little knowledge of the country's cuisine. To say it was nerve-wracking is an understatement—for the first six months, I worked for free, spoke to no one, and had only Sunday evenings off—these would be the most challenging and loneliest couple of years of my life, but it was an experience I will never regret undertaking. The cuisine at El Cenador de Salvador was a perfect blend of classic Spanish cuisine and modern Spanish molecular gastronomy, and the knowledge I gained there was invaluable.

Following that I did a *stage* at Arzak, a three-Michelin-star restaurant in San Sebastián, one of the first and oldest three-star restaurants outside of France, and another revolutionary place that brought molecular and Spanish gastronomy to the world stage. I learned a lot from my time at Arzak and fell in love with San Sebastián, its amazing food and drink as well as its natural beauty.

After spending two years in Spain, I had an opportunity to return to London to work in what would be the most influential restaurant experience of my career. Pearl Restaurant in Holborn, located in the

Chancery Court Hotel, was led by Chef Jun Tanaka. When I interviewed there, I knew within the first hour that I had to stay. The food was fresh, immaculate, and unique, the kitchen was like a well-oiled machine; it was intense and every minute was precious, but it was a real team effort—we started at the same time and finished at the same time. All the chefs, managers, and waiters were on the same page, we all wanted the same result, so it made the long hours and all the effort worthwhile. I was fortunate to work with some amazing chefs during my time there; James Lawrence, Ben Knell, and Chef Tanaka all had a massive impact on my career. Jun was a true leader, he was the fastest, cleanest, most efficient of all of us, none of us could keep up with him, and I believe if you're going to call yourself the head chef, then you should be the best in the kitchen and set an example every day—this was the most important lesson I took away from Pearl, and something I try to emulate every day in my own kitchen. These were long, tough days, but I would go back to work with this team any day—to find a group of such dedicated, talented chefs all in the same kitchen at the same time is a rare thing.

At this point, my talented wife had a job offer in New York and Tanaka recommended me for a position at Gordon Ramsey's new restaurant in the London Hotel in Manhattan. After six months we received two Michelin stars. From there I received an offer from Hakkasan Group, a global Michelin-starred restaurant group, to open their flagship restaurant in New York City. Hakkasan began in London many years before; it was the first Asian restaurant to receive a Michelin star in Europe. Its creator Alan Yau is an amazing innovator, who is also behind brands such as Yauatcha and Wagamama. What I love most about his restaurants is the attention to detail; the smallest thing, something the clientele would probably not even notice, is considered. After a bumpy start, six months later we received our first Michelin star, no easy feat in New York City. I was very fortunate to work with some incredible people there, Chef Ho Chee Boon and Graham Hornigold, as well as the teams in each of their many locations around the United States, which I went on to oversee.

After fours years of traveling and restaurant openings for the Hakkasan Group, I finally had the opportunity to pursue my personal dream of having my own place in New York City. Patisserie Chanson and Dessert Bar had been years in the making, and to open a new business in the most competitive city in the world is difficult, so the fact that we even managed to get both floors operating is something I will always be proud of. I wanted to bring my version of the patisserie to Manhattan—not the classic French variety but a combination of European styles, not gimmicky but modern, high end but approachable. And the dessert bar, my pride and joy, I had been dreaming of for years: a chef's table-style bar where we create everything in front of you and give you an experience instead of a meal, where hospitality is the most important aspect, inviting guests to see and interact with us and providing a stage on which to create something truly unique.

This book includes all of my favorite recipes from Chanson and throughout my career. I hope you get the same enjoyment out of them as I still do every day.

A DAY AS A PASTRY CHEF

First in, last out.

That's the first thing I say to anyone looking to enter this profession. In a restaurant the pastry chefs are the beginning and the end of a meal, and in patisseries or bakeries, their work often starts just as everyone else goes to bed.

It can be tough and relentless, but I have never thought of it as a sacrifice. Whether working as a chef or a pastry chef, this is my job, this is what I do. And if you want to have any sort of success in this career, you have to work hard and be dedicated. It's not glamorous, but it is rewarding. It's the little things: I still smile every time I tap out a tray of shiny chocolate bonbons, and I'm still proud when my macarons come out with perfectly straight sides or when I speak with a guest who enjoyed their pastry. As Chef Evans taught me, success is not about recognition, success is about being proud of what you do. And that's true for the recipes in this book. Practice until you get them right, and then take pride in the results, whether it's a caramel or a croissant, in a professional kitchen or at home.

RULES FOR PERFECT PASTRY

Pastry making is a discipline. The more you can stick to the rules, the greater your chance of consistency and success. In my kitchen if a cook says to me, "Something went wrong, I don't know what happened, I did everything the same," we backtrack and look at each step of the process because that's not how baking works, especially when it comes to pastry. At some point the rules weren't followed, whether it was the scaling of the recipe, the time of a proof, the temperature or baking time or fan speed of the oven, something was different and it had an effect. When it comes to baking, there is something really satisfying, almost addictive, to following the rules, because that way you will get the same results every time.

This may sound a little daunting, but once you have mastered the following rules, you will have the knowledge you need to change them. A great example of this is my croissant recipe on page 41. Once you have mastered this recipe, the possibilities are endless, from chocolate-raspberry or pistachio to black truffle and prosciutto croissants, all using the same base dough.

CLEANLINESS

Cleanliness is paramount. In the kitchen it's actually the most important aspect of our work—if your work area is dirty, then your food is dirty. This is the first and most important thing a young cook will learn and it will serve them for the rest of their career. The same should be applied to a home cook, too. Being clean and organized will make baking more efficient, less stressful, and more enjoyable—and that's how baking should be!

• Before starting any recipe, empty your dishwasher or fill your sink with soapy water, so you can clean up as you go. This will keep your work surfaces clear, and when you have finished baking, you can sit back and enjoy your creation without an hour's worth of cleaning ahead of you.

• Clear as much counter space as possible; this will help you to keep things clean and organized as you cook.

• Get all the necessary equipment out, and have it clean and ready before you start. This way you won't be stressing out as you search in the back of your cupboards halfway through a recipe.

WEIGH YOUR INGREDIENTS

There are many variables in baking—adding the precise quantity of ingredients called for in a recipe should not be one of them. As every good pastry chef knows, weighing items, preferably on a digital kitchen scale, is the cleanest, fastest, most efficient, and most importantly, accurate method for achieving this. That is why I strongly recommend that you get into the habit of weighing your ingredients rather than measuring them using cups and tablespoons.

Here are some examples that demonstrate how weighing can make all the difference when it comes to the success of your pastries, breads, and other baked goods:

• One cup of flour might weigh 50 percent more than another, depending on how it is scooped or packed.

• Different brands of salt are not equal when measured by volume, so depending on the salt you are using (Morton versus fine sea salt, for example), you could be adding too much or too little, potentially a significant variable, especially when we are dealing with the laminated doughs and pastry in this book.

• Eggs are another massive variable: depending on where you buy them, the weight of six large eggs can vary by as much as 200 grams (that's 7 ounces).

Be disciplined when weighing the ingredients called for in the recipes that follow, and you can be confident of getting the same result each time: perfection!

That said, I recognize that not every home baker is ready to commit to weighing all of their ingredients. Because of this I've included imperial volume measures alongside the metric weights. Here are a few suggestions to help offset the error involved in the scenarios described above:

• When measuring flour, confectioners' sugar, or cocoa powder, lightly spoon it into the measuring cup—rather than packing it in or dipping and sweeping the cup through the flour to measure it.

• I've used regular table salt, such as Morton or kosher salt, in all of the recipes in this book, plus occasionally a flaky sea salt like Maldon or fleur de sel for finishing. If you do the same, you'll add the correct amount of salt.

• In addition to providing total grams for eggs, egg whites, and egg yolks, I've provided *both* tablespoon/cup equivalents and the approximate number of eggs

you will need to achieve these measures. This way if you discover that these measures aren't precisely in accord with the eggs you typically buy, you can adjust the volume measures accordingly.

Please keep in mind that the imperial measures provided are approximate. Based on outcomes, you may decide to make some tweaks to the quantities called for in a recipe the next time you prepare it. Although weighing is more foolproof, this process of making adjustments will teach you a lot about baking. Make notes for yourself in the margins of the recipes or on sticky notes!

OVEN HOT SPOTS

Every oven is different and will have hot spots—even convection ovens will have these. So, it is worth your while to try to figure out where they are and how that might affect your baking. In this book, I have provided baking times and temperatures based on the oven I have at home rather than the one I use in a professional kitchen. Some recipes may require a little trial and error, but don't give up—you can only succeed through failure.

EXOPAT

ATFER　MADE IN FRANCE　L 20

"IF IT AIN'T BROKE, DON'T FIX IT"

This saying is something I think about every day in the kitchen.

"Do we need to change this recipe?"
"Is this better now that we've changed it?"

I ask these questions whenever we are testing a new recipe. Did we improve it or are we just changing it because we're bored of making the same thing every day?

Here's another way of saying it: "Respect the old but embrace the new." If you master the classics, then the possibilities are endless. Each chapter of this book starts with a base recipe: learn how to make a beautiful croissant and then you can move on to raspberry and chocolate croissants; start with the basic choux pastry and end up with Paris-Brest Éclairs.

Baking is a skill, a trade, an art form—whatever you want to call it, baking takes time, patience, and practice. Don't be disheartened if your first round of macarons doesn't rise, or if your first attempt at croissants doesn't look like the photos. Examine all the variables and see if there was anything you missed so you can come up with a plan for the next round. It can be frustrating, but don't give up— when you bite into a perfect macaron or croissant that you made yourself, that feeling will far outshine any frustration.

Happy baking!

MY GRANNY'S SCONES

MAKES 20 SCONES

My granny (like most grandmothers of her generation) was an amazing cook. She grew up in a time of rationing and perpetual struggle, but even with the most basic ingredients, she had a way of making everything taste delicious. (There were never any leftovers at Granny's house.) Although my scones could never compete with hers, I decided to make the first recipe in this book my take on her scones. This recipe embodies the maxim, simplicity isn't always simple, but it is always the best—and incredibly tasty, too!

In a stand mixer with a paddle attachment, combine the flour, sugar, baking powder, and butter. Mix on a medium speed until the mixture develops a sandy texture. Transfer the bowl to the refrigerator and allow the mixture to rest for 1 hour.

Return the bowl to the mixer. In a separate bowl, whisk together the milk and eggs. With the machine running on a low speed, gently pour the egg mixture into the flour and butter mixture and mix until it just comes together. Add the raisins to the dough and mix for 1 minute, just until combined.

On a lightly floured work surface, gently knead the dough, shaping it into a ball, and wrap in plastic wrap. Refrigerate for 1 hour.

Remove the dough from the plastic wrap and place it on a work surface that has been lightly dusted with flour.

Using a rolling pin, roll out the dough until about 3/4 inch thick. Using a 2 1/2-inch ring cutter, punch out 20 scones and place them on a half-sheet pan lined with parchment paper or a silicone mat (see Sources, page 251). Allow to rest for at least 30 minutes in the refrigerator.

Meanwhile, preheat your oven to 375°F (if you have a convection oven, set it on fan speed 2).

In a small bowl, make the egg wash by whisking together the egg and milk until combined, which should take about 30 seconds.

Brush the tops of the scones with egg wash and bake for 10 minutes, until they are golden brown on top. Allow the scones to cool on a wire rack before serving.

INGREDIENT	WEIGHT	VOLUME
all-purpose flour, preferably King Arthur Sir Galahad artisan flour	1 kilogram	8 1/3 cups
sugar	188 grams	15 tablespoons
baking powder	55 grams	3 tablespoons + 2 teaspoons
lightly salted European butter, such as Beurre d'Isigny, at room temperature	250 grams	1 cup + 2 tablespoons
milk	370 grams	1 1/2 cups
4 large eggs	200 grams	3/4 cup + 2 teaspoons
raisins	100 grams	2/3 cup
egg wash (50 grams/1 egg to 2 tablespoons milk)	--------	--------

TIP: Rest the dough three times to achieve scones that will stay light and fluffy. Resting in between processes allows the gluten strands to relax so they are not tight and compact when baked.

TIP: Although not vital, convection ovens are preferred for the recipes in this book—the reason being the fans and settings in a convection oven allow the heat to be transferred more evenly, resulting in more even cooking throughout the oven. Traditional ovens tend to have hot spots, normally on the bottom or at the back of the oven—if this is the case with your oven, more careful monitoring of the baked goods and regular rotation of the pans may be required.

MORNING PROVISIONS

The smell of a freshly baked croissant, just out of the oven, is for me one of the best feelings in the world and immediately takes me to my childhood memories of Paris. I am lucky to work in a kitchen where we experience this every morning; my hope is that the recipes in this chapter will allow you to enjoy this simple pleasure in your kitchen too. Personally I am not a fan of overly sweet pastries, especially for breakfast, so I avoid using any icing or very sweet jams or fillings. The dough is sweet enough on its own, so I try to balance the sweetness of any filling rather than enhance it. The lemon and poppy seed kouign-amann (page 65) is a great example of this—the lemon curd is tart and the poppy seeds add a savory flavor; when you combine them with the rich, sweet dough, you achieve a perfect balance.

Like all the recipes in this book, the pastry recipes in this chapter are designed to be versatile. Master the technique for making croissants and you will have a whole range of sweet and savory options you can make and even ideas for using any leftover croissants for the next day. Some of my favorite recipes here are for kouign-amanns, a classic pastry from the Breton region in France that has seen a revival in the last couple of years; once you try one, you'll wonder why they are not as popular as croissants! When making kouign-amanns, sugar is sprinkled over the croissant dough on the last fold and in some cases that dough is piped with filling, then it is baked in muffin tins, resulting in a caramelized sugar crust. I call them the "croissant's favorite cousin" for this exact reason—they are similiar yet totally unique.

This chapter offers a wide range of sweet and savory options, depending on your preference, moving into brunch ideas where there are some simple, hand-mixed breads. The nice thing with these recipes is again the versatility: one base recipe of ciabatta can give you ciabatta rolls, focaccia, pizza bianca, and much more—the possibilities are endless.

THE BELOVED CROISSANT

The croissant. So iconic, the good, the bad, the ugly, we have probably had all of them at some point. This pastry is now a breakfast staple worldwide, but how often do people think of the bakers starting work at 1 a.m., laminating dough, shaping, proofing and baking so your croissant is ready when you walk in for your morning coffee? If this was more common knowledge, I am certain people would take a closer look at those hard-earned layers, the texture of the crust, how flaky it is when you take your first bite.

Whenever I try a croissant, I always judge it on how messy I am; if the table and I are both covered in flakes, then I know I am on to a winner. Ask yourself if you can taste the butter or just fat, is it greasy or rich, moist or dry? Such a humble pastry goes through so much before it hits the counter, but it is the basis of almost all of what we call viennoiserie. These are generally breakfast pastries made with laminated dough. By laminated, I am describing the process of creating layers of butter and dough, repeatedly—it is these layers that give the humble croissant its shape, flavor, and texture, and learning this technique is the basis of this chapter.

When making any of the recipes in this chapter, time and patience are key; some are a two-day process, and all need to be kept cold so the layers of dough and butter remain distinct. Avoid the urge to rush through this process, take your time and be rewarded with the satisfaction of a perfectly baked croissant.

LAMINATED DOUGH

Laminating dough refers to the process of repeatedly folding butter into a dough, thus creating the very thin alternating layers of butter and dough that we savor in croissants and other flaky, buttery pastries like the kouign-amann featured in the next chapter.

POOLISH STARTER

INGREDIENT	WEIGHT	VOLUME
all-purpose flour, preferably King Arthur brand	100 grams	13 tablespoons
instant yeast, SAF gold label	0.2 gram	1 pinch
water at 75°F	100 grams	7 tablespoons

In a bowl, combine the flour and yeast and mix them with your fingers until well combined. Gradually pour in the water and continue to mix with your fingers until there are no lumps.

Cover the bowl loosely with plastic wrap and let it sit at room temperature for 12 to 15 hours. The mixture should bubble when it's ready.

TIP: If the starter has not started to ferment or bubble on its own, the best thing to do is to start again with new yeast and make sure the water is the correct temperature—if it's too hot it will kill the yeast and nothing will happen.

BUTTER BLOCK

INGREDIENT	WEIGHT	VOLUME
European unsalted butter shaped into a rectangle *(see page 34)*, soft enough to leave your fingerprint in *(ideally 1 hour at normal room temperature)*	500 grams	2 1/4 cups

Spread out a piece of parchment paper on a work surface and then place the butter in the center. Top with another piece of parchment paper and, using a rolling pin, pound the butter as evenly as possible—the end result should be an even rectangle approximately 6 3/4 by 7 1/2 inches. Rotate the butter block 90 degrees and continue pounding with the rolling pin until this rectangle shape is achieved. (If you prefer you can find a rectangular frame in most kitchen supply stores.) Wrap in the parchment paper and store in the refrigerator.

CROISSANT DOUGH

INGREDIENT	WEIGHT	VOLUME
bread flour, preferably King Arthur Special Patent	400 grams	3 cups + 1 tablespoon
all-purpose flour, preferably King Arthur Sir Galahad artisan flour, plus more for shaping the dough	400 grams	3 1/3 cups
whole-wheat flour, preferably King Arthur brand	60 grams	scant 1/2 cup
sugar	75 grams	6 tablespoons
instant yeast, SAF gold label	15 grams	4 1/4 teaspoons
poolish starter (page 32)	172 grams	1 3/4 cups
milk	500 grams	2 cups + 1 tablespoon
unsalted butter, at room temperature	80 grams	6 tablespoons
salt	30 grams	4 1/2 teaspoons

TIP: Making laminated dough is a detailed process, but this base recipe can be used to make all the recipes in this chapter, so stick with it. This dough can be frozen for up to 1 week.

Combine the flours, sugar, and yeast in the bowl of a stand mixer fitted with a dough hook and give it a quick mix to combine. Add the poolish, milk, and the butter and mix on a low speed for 2 minutes. Scrape the bottom of the bowl with a spatula to make sure all the flour is combined.

Sprinkle the salt on top of the dough and continue to mix for 2 minutes; if the dough is looking dry at this point, add a little bit of water. Mix on low speed for another 20 minutes, until the dough comes away from the mixing bowl and forms a ball and the sides of the bowl are clean.

TIP: Mix this dough for a long time so the gluten strands develop and are strong—this will then allow you to stretch and roll out the dough and shape the croissants.

Using a bench knife, scrape the dough out onto a lightly floured surface. Imagine that you are folding a letter to put in an envelope. Take the left side of the dough, stretch it, and bring it into the center of the dough, then stretch and fold the right side over to the opposite side. Repeat this process, this time working from the bottom and then the top.

Line a half-sheet pan with parchment paper. Carefully place the dough on a lightly floured work surface. Without stretching the dough, gently but firmly pat the dough into a 10 by 8-inch rectangle using a rolling pin. Transfer to the prepared pan and place in the freezer for 20 minutes.

BUTTER LOCK-IN

Turn the dough out onto a lightly floured work surface and lightly flour the top.

Using a rolling pin, roll the dough outward from its center, rotating and flipping it frequently and adding just enough flour to keep it from sticking. Your goal is to create a 16 by 8 by 1/2-inch rectangle.

Place the chilled butter block directly in the middle of the rectangle. Fold each side of the dough into the center and pinch them together, so you cannot see any of the butter from above.

Using a rolling pin, press down firmly on the dough across the seam, rolling from one side to another. Then turn the dough 90 degrees so the short side faces you, and this time roll away from you. Continue to flip and rotate the dough, adding flour as necessary to keep it from sticking to the table, until you have a 22 by 9 by 3/8-inch rectangle.

Fold the bottom third of the dough up as if you were folding a letter, fold the top third down to cover the bottom third, then turn the block 90 degrees as if it were a book, with the opening on the right. This completes the first turn: Mark it by making a thumbprint in the dough, return the dough to the half-sheet pan, cover it with plastic, and put it in the freezer for 20 minutes.

Repeat this process two more times, for a total of three turns.

TIP: Note that this dough is kept cold throughout; however, if the butter block starts to crack, or the dough does not roll smoothly, it means the temperature is too cold; give the dough a few minutes to soften before resuming.

FINISH THE DOUGH

Remove the dough from the freezer and place it on the lightly floured surface with the opening on the right.

Roll the dough out until you have a 24 by 9-inch rectangle. Cut the dough crosswise to make two 12 by 9-inch rectangles.

Stack the two rectangles on top of each other and freeze for 20 minutes, or until the dough is firm again. The dough is now ready.

LAMINATED
DOUGH

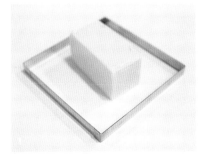  

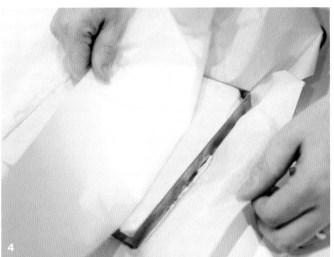

1 Begin making the "butter block"

2 Using a rolling pin, pound the butter or push it into a frame

3 Make the butter block as square and as even as possible and place in the fridge

4 Once set, remove the paper and the frame if used

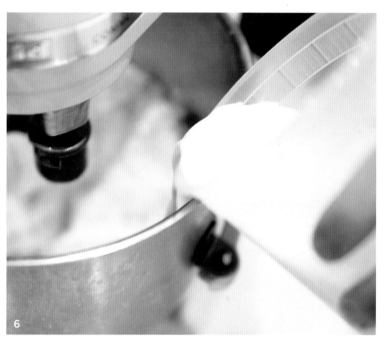

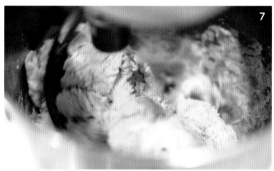

5 Begin making the dough,
combining flours, sugar, and yeast

6 Add the milk, poolish, and butter

7 Begin to mix with a dough hook

8 Mix until it becomes a smooth dough

LAMINATED DOUGH

9 Place the dough on a lightly floured surface

10 Begin to stretch the dough

11 Transfer the dough to a half-sheet pan, pat down with a rolling pin, and chill

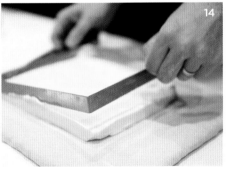

12 Begin rolling the dough, ready for the butter "lock-in"

13 Shape into a rectangle

14 Add the butter block to the dough

15 Stretch the dough and fold over the butter

16 Cover the butter with the dough

17 Pinch dough seam together until the butter is totally sealed, and trim any excess that does not contain butter

LAMINATED
DOUGH

18 Begin to roll the dough from the center out

19 Letter fold the dough

20 Gently push down the dough with a rolling pin

21 Repeat the process; now the laminated dough is ready

22 If making croissants, cut the dough into triangles

23 Stretch the dough triangles so they are one-third longer

24 Starting from the widest end, roll the dough triangles

25 Place the croissant on a half-sheet pan and press down slightly to seal the tip in place

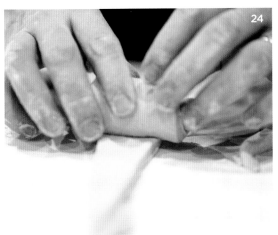

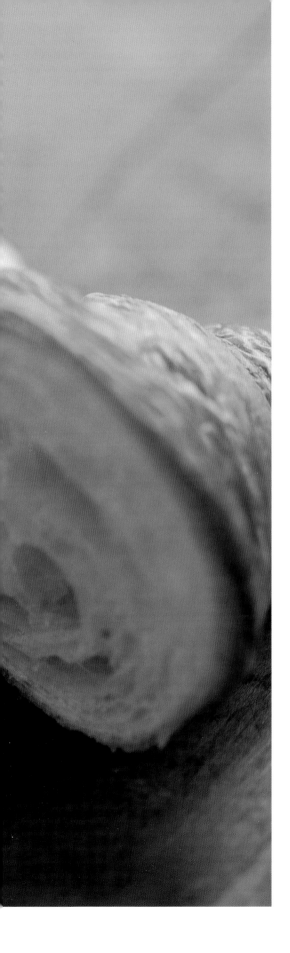

CROISSANT AU BEURRE
MAKES 16 CROISSANTS

This is the classic—crisp buttery layers of yeast dough in a straight-sided spiral shape. Traditionally, croissants au beurre have straight sides while regular croissants, which are made with margarine, have that more iconic crescent shape. This practice comes from a time in France during and soon after World War II when butter was not readily available, so margarine was used as a cheaper replacement; the two shapes were meant to signify the difference.

Spray two half-sheet pans with nonstick cooking spray and line them with parchment paper.

Lightly flour your work surface. Remove one piece of laminated dough (see page 32) from the freezer. With a short end toward you, roll the dough into a rectangle that's approximately 19 by 9 inches.

Turn the dough so a long side is facing you and trim it so it's 18 inches long. Trim the other three edges so they are straight. (You can put the trimmings in a resealable plastic bag and reserve them in the freezer.)

Working quickly, starting on the left side, measure 4 inches along the bottom edge of the rectangle of dough and cut from this point to the top-left corner to make a triangle. For the second triangle, measure 4 inches along the top of the rectangle and cut straight down. Repeat this process until you have 16 triangles of dough.

Holding the base of one of the triangles of dough, gently pull the triangle down, stretching to increase the length by around a third.

Lay the triangle back down on the table, and starting at the base roll up the triangle to form a spiral. Place on one of the prepared pans and press down lightly to seal the tip of the croissant in place.

TIP: *Sealing the tip is an important step so the croissants won't unfurl during proofing or baking.*

Repeat this process with the rest of the triangles of dough.

Brush the croissants with egg wash (see page 27), cover them with cardboard or plastic boxes, and allow to proof for about 2 hours; they should double in size.

Brush the croissants with egg wash again and preheat the oven to 350°F.

Bake for 25 minutes, until the croissants are a deep golden brown. Check on them after 10 minutes—if they are getting too much color, reduce the temperature to 325°F.

Set the pans on a wire rack and let cool completely.

CHOCOLATINE
MAKES 16 CHOCOLATINES

This is a great alternative to the classic pain au chocolat—the addition of cocoa powder in the dough and on top gives this pastry a slight bitterness that I really love. Served fresh and warm out of the oven, there is nothing better.

In the bowl of a stand mixer fitted with a dough hook, combine the flours, sugar, cocoa powder, and yeast and give them a quick mix to combine.

Add the poolish, milk (reserving 50 grams or 3 1/3 tablespoons), and butter to the flour mixture. Mix on a low speed for 2 minutes, scraping the bottom of the bowl to make sure all the flour is combined.

Sprinkle the salt on top of the dough and continue to mix for 2 minutes. If the dough is looking dry, add a little bit of water. Continue to mix on low speed for 20 minutes.

Using a pastry scraper, scrape the dough out onto a lightly floured work surface.

Imagine you are folding a letter to put in an envelope: Take the left side of the dough, stretch it and bring it into the center of the dough, then stretch and fold the right side over to the opposite side. Repeat the process, working from the bottom and then the top.

Turn the dough over and place it on a lightly floured half-sheet pan. Cover with plastic wrap and let rest at room temperature for 1 hour.

Line a half-sheet pan with parchment paper. Carefully transfer the dough to a lightly floured work surface. Without stretching the dough, gently but firmly pat it into a 10 by 8-inch rectangle using a rolling pin. Transfer to the prepared pan and put in the freezer for 20 minutes.

Once the dough has chilled, follow the butter lock-in process described for the croissant au beurre on page 33 to create laminated dough.

When you're ready to shape the chocolatines, spray two half-sheet pans with nonstick spray and line them with parchment paper.

Remove one piece of laminated dough and place it on a lightly floured work surface, with a short end toward you. Roll out the dough into a rectangle about 19 by 9 inches.

INGREDIENT	WEIGHT	VOLUME
all-purpose flour, preferably King Arthur brand	480 grams	4 cups
bread flour, preferably King Arthur Special Patent	480 grams	3 2/3 cups
sugar	115 grams	9 tablespoons
unsweetened cocoa powder, such as Valrhona brand, plus more for dusting	125 grams	1 cup
instant yeast, SAF gold label	17 grams	4 3/4 teaspoons
poolish starter (page 32)	190 grams	scant 2 cups
milk	645 grams	2 2/3 cups
lightly salted European butter, such as Beurre D'Isgny	95 grams	7 tablespoons
fine sea salt	25 grams	5 1/2 teaspoons
64 Valrhona dark chocolate bâtons (55 percent cacao; see Sources, page 250)	--------	4 batons per chocolatine
egg wash (1 egg/50 grams to 2 tablespoons milk)	--------	--------

Turn the dough so a long side is facing you and trim it so it is 18 inches long. Trim the other edges so they are straight. Reserve the trimmings in a zip-tight bag in the freezer.

Working quickly, starting on the left edge measure 4-inch squares (see step-by-step photo, page 60). On each square of pastry, 1 inch up from the bottom, lay two chocolate batons followed by another two batons 1 inch above the previous pair—four batons total for each chocolatine.

Starting from the bottom and moving up, roll the dough over the first two batons to cover them and then over again to cover the second two batons. You should have somewhat of a spiral, with four batons encased in it. Repeat the process with the remaining squares of dough and chocolate batons.

Arrange the chocolatines on the prepared pans, leaving space in between the pastries. Cover them with cardboard or plastic boxes, and allow to proof for about 2 hours; they should double in size.

Preheat the oven to 350°F.

Brush the chocolatines with egg wash. Bake for 25 minutes, until they turn a deep golden brown color. Check on them after 10 minutes—if they are getting too much color, reduce the temperature to 325°F.

When the chocolatines come out of the oven, dust them with additional cocoa powder. Set the pans on a wire rack and allow the pastries to cool completely.

CHOCOLATE & RASPBERRY CROISSANTS

MAKES 16 CROISSANTS

Raspberries and chocolate are a match made in culinary heaven. Here a plain croissant dough and a red dough are spiraled together to encase a raspberry chocolate ganache that will be revealed at the first bite. If you don't have time to make the red dough, the flavor of dark chocolate and raspberry ganache is more than enough.

Make the ganache: Melt the chocolate in a metal bowl over simmering water.

In a bowl, combine the egg whites, confectioners' sugar, flour, salt, and raspberry purée and whisk until combined and free of lumps.

Pour in the melted chocolate and immediately whisk to keep the chocolate from seizing up and continue until there are no lumps.

Spoon into a piping bag and reserve.

Prepare the red dough: In a stand mixer with the dough hook attachment, mix the croissant dough with the food coloring until it is a solid red color throughout. On a lightly floured surface, roll the dough into a rectangle that's approximately 19 by 9 inches. Trim the edges to make it 18 inches long. Reserve in the freezer.

Spray two half-sheet pans with nonstick spray and line with parchment paper.

Assemble the croissants: Lightly flour your work surface. Remove one piece of laminated dough from the freezer. With a short end toward you, roll the dough into a rectangle that's approximately 19 by 9 inches.

Turn the dough so a long side is facing you and trim it so it's 18 inches long. Trim the other three edges so they are straight. (You can put the trimmings in a resealable plastic bag and reserve them in the freezer.)

Take the red dough from the freezer and place it directly on top of the croissant dough.

Working quickly, starting on the left side, measure 4 inches along the bottom edge of the rectangle of dough and cut from this point to the top-left corner to make a triangle (see step-by-step photo, page 39). For the second triangle, measure 4 inches along the top of the rectangle and cut straight down. Repeat this process until you have 16 triangles of dough.

INGREDIENT	WEIGHT	VOLUME
Raspberry Chocolate Ganache		
baking chocolate	250 grams or	-------
(see Sources, page 250)	8 3/4 ounces	
6 1/2 large egg whites	200 grams	13 tablespoons
confectioners' sugar	300 grams	2 1/2 cups
all-purpose flour, preferably	40 grams	1/3 cup
King Arthur Galahad		
artisan flour		
salt	3 grams	1/2 teaspoon
raspberry purée	100 grams	7 tablespoons
(see Sources, page 251)		
Red Dough		
unlaminated Croissant Dough	340 grams	1/3 of base croissant
(page 33)		dough recipe
red liquid food coloring	15 grams	3 teaspoons
(see Sources, page 250)		
2 blocks (12 x 9 inches each)	--------	--------
laminated Croissant Dough		
(page 32)		
egg wash (1 egg/50 grams	--------	--------
to 2 tablespoons milk)		
freeze-dried raspberries,	--------	--------
for garnish		

Holding the base of one of the triangles of dough, gently pull the triangle down, stretching to increase the length by around a third (see photo, page 39).

Lay out one of the triangles on the work surface and pipe a 3 1/2-inch stripe of the raspberry chocolate ganache along the base of the triangle. Starting at the base, roll up the triangle to form a spiral. Place on one of the prepared pans and press down lightly to seal the tip of the croissant in place. Repeat this process with the rest of the dough triangles and the ganache.

NOTE: Sealing the tip is an important step so the croissants won't unfurl during proofing or baking.

Brush the croissants with egg wash (page 27), cover them with cardboard or plastic boxes, and allow to proof for about 2 hours; they should double in size.

Brush the croissants with egg wash again and preheat the oven to 350°F.

Bake for 25 minutes, until the croissants are a deep golden brown. Check on them after 10 minutes—if they are getting too much color, reduce the temperature to 325°F.

Set the pans on a wire rack and garnish the croissants with the freeze-dried raspberries, then let cool completely.

SICILIAN PISTACHIO CROISSANTS

MAKES 16 CROISSANTS

Sicilian pistachios, grown in the foothills of Mount Etna, have long been revered for their sweet, richly concentrated flavor. These croissants fill spirals of plain and green dough with a cream made from this distinctive and delicious ingredient.

Make the pastry cream: In a saucepan, whisk together the milk, cream, salt, and pistachio pastes and bring to a boil. Mix together the sugar with the cornstarch until well combined. In a bowl, whisk together the egg yolks with the sugar and cornstarch mixture.

When the milk boils, slowly pour it over the egg mixture, whisking continually, then return it to the pot. Bring to a boil and whisk until the custard thickens. Reduce the heat and cook for another minute, whisking vigorously. At this stage it is very important that you do not stop whisking until the mixture has thickened; if you do the eggs may scramble.

Put the custard into the bowl of a stand mixer and mix for 5 minutes, then allow to cool slightly before adding the cubed butter and mix until the custard has fully thickened. Pour it into a plastic container and cover with plastic wrap so it's touching the surface of the custard. Let cool in the refrigerator until needed.

Prepare the green dough: In a stand mixer with a dough hook, mix the croissant dough with the food coloring until it is a solid green color throughout. On a lightly floured surface, roll the dough into a rectangle that's approximately 19 by 9 inches. Trim the edges to make it 18 inches. Reserve in the freezer.

Spray two half-sheet pans with nonstick spray and line with parchment paper.

Assemble the croissants: Lightly flour your work surface. Remove one piece of laminated dough from the freezer. With a short end toward you, roll the dough into a rectangle that's approximately 19 by 9 inches.

Turn the dough so a long side is facing you and trim it so it's 18 inches long. Trim the other three edges so they are straight. (You can put the trimmings in a resealable plastic bag and reserve them in the freezer.)

Take the green dough from the freezer and place it directly on top of the croissant dough.

Working quickly, starting on the left side, measure

INGREDIENT	WEIGHT	VOLUME
Sicilian Pistachio Pastry Cream		
milk	320 grams	1 1/3 cups
heavy cream	320 grams	1 cup + 6 tablespoons
natural pistachio paste (see Sources, page 251)	40 grams	8 teaspoons
sweetened pistachio paste (see Sources, page 251)	50 grams	10 teaspoons
salt	3 grams	1/2 teaspoon
sugar	160 grams	13 tablespoons
cornstarch	45 grams	1/3 cup
7 egg yolks	130 grams	1/2 cup
cold unsalted European-style butter, cut into cubes	80 grams	5 1/2 tablespoons
Green Dough		
unlaminated Croissant Dough (page 33)	340 grams	1/3 of the base croissant dough recipe
green food coloring	15 grams	3 teaspoons
2 blocks (12 x 9 inches each) laminated Croissant Dough (page 32)	--------	--------
egg wash (1 egg/50 grams to 2 tablespoons milk)	--------	--------

4 inches along the bottom edge of the rectangle of dough and cut from this point to the top-left corner to make a triangle. For the second triangle, measure 4 inches along the top of the rectangle and cut straight down. Repeat this process until you have 16 triangles of dough.

Holding the base of one of the triangles of dough, gently pull the triangle down, stretching to increase the length by around a third.

Lay out one of the triangles on the work surface and pipe a 3 1/2-inch strip of the pistachio pastry cream along the base of the triangle. Starting at the base, roll up the triangle to form a spiral. Place on one of the prepared pans and press down lightly to seal the tip of the croissant in place. Repeat this process with the rest of the dough triangles and the pastry cream.

NOTE: Sealing the tip is an important step so the croissants won't unfurl during proofing or baking.

Brush the croissants with egg wash, cover them with cardboard or plastic boxes, and allow to proof for about 2 hours; they should double in size.

Brush the croissants with egg wash again and preheat the oven to 350°F.

Bake for 25 minutes, until the croissants are a deep golden brown. Check on them after 10 minutes—if they are getting too much color, reduce the temperature to 325°F.

Set the pans on a wire rack and let cool completely.

EVERYTHING CROISSANTS
MAKES 16 CROISSANTS

A modern take on that classic New York City staple, the everything bagel. When you can't decide which bagel to get, go for one with everything on it. The same goes for croissants now. This recipe shows the versatility of the croissant, which can be part of a savory breakfast too. The best thing about this recipe is that it's a self-contained breakfast; no need to add anything, unless you want extra jalapeño cream cheese!

INGREDIENT	WEIGHT	VOLUME
Jalapeño Cream Cheese		
cream cheese	250 grams	1 cup
jalapeño pepper, minced	50 grams	1/3 cup
Everything Mix: 1:1		
poppy seeds	50 grams	1/3 cup
onion flakes	50 grams	3 tablespoons
white sesame seeds	50 grams	1/3 cup
dry garlic	50 grams	2 tablespoons
Maldon salt, or other flaky sea salt	50 grams	3 tablespoons
2 blocks (12 x 9 inches each) laminated Croissant Dough (page 32)	--------	--------

In a bowl, beat together the cream cheese and jalapeño until fully combined and the cream cheese has softened slightly. Reserve in a piping bag.

Mix the everything-mix ingredients together and store in an airtight container.

Spray two half-sheet pans with nonstick spray and line with parchment paper.

Lay out 16 prepared croissant dough triangles (see page 33). Hold the base of each one, gently pulling it down, stretching the dough to increase its length by about a third.

Pipe a 3 1/2 inch strip of the jalapeño cream cheese mixture at the base of each croissant triangle.

Starting at the base, roll up the triangle to form a spiral. Place on one of the prepared half-sheet pans and press down lightly to seal the tip of the croissant in place. Repeat this process with the rest of the dough triangles and cream cheese mixture.

Brush the croissants with egg wash (see page 27) and then liberally sprinkle with the everything mix so the whole croissant has an even layer of the mix. Cover the croissants with cardboard or plastic boxes and allow to proof for about 2 hours or until they have doubled in size.

Preheat the oven to 350°F. Bake for 25 minutes, until the croissants are a deep golden brown; check on them after 10 minutes, and if they are getting too much color, reduce the temperature to 325°F.

Set pans on a wire rack and allow to cool completely.

CROQUE MONSIEUR CROISSANTS

MAKES 4 SANDWICHES

This is a great way to use any croissants that are left over the next day; all that effort should never go to waste. Warm these sandwiches slightly in the oven before serving for a perfect lunch.

INGREDIENT	WEIGHT	VOLUME
4 fresh or day-old croissants	--------	--------
whole-grain mustard	50 grams	1 teaspoon per sandwich
Béchamel Sauce (recipe opposite)	120 grams	2 tablespoons per sandwich
4 slices black forest ham	2 to 3 ounces	--------
4 slices aged cheddar	2 to 3 ounces	--------
4 rosemary sprigs	--------	--------

Preheat the oven to 350°F.

Slice the croissants in half lengthwise and spread a thin layer of mustard on both halves.

On the bottom halves of the croissants, spread a thick layer of béchamel sauce, then add one slice of ham, folded in half, and one slice of cheddar to each.

Add the tops of the croissants and secure each sandwich through the middle with a rosemary sprig.

Bake for 10 minutes and enjoy them while they're hot.

BÉCHAMEL SAUCE

INGREDIENT	WEIGHT	VOLUME
olive oil	120 grams	9 tablespoons
butter	120 grams	generous 1/2 cup
1/2 onion, chopped	52 to 65 grams	6 tablespoons to 1/2 cup
bread flour, preferably King Arthur Special Patent	206 grams	1 cup + 9 tablespoons
salt	12 grams	1 3/4 teaspoons
1/2 nutmeg, freshly grated	--------	--------
milk	1.95 kilograms	8 cups

Melt the oil and butter in a saucepan over a medium heat. Add the onion and sauté for 1 minute. Add the flour, salt, and nutmeg and whisk for 4 minutes, until it comes together to look like a paste. Continue to cook over a low heat for 5 to 8 minutes, until the raw flour taste is cooked out. Pour in the milk and whisk continually until the sauce comes to a boil.

If not using immediately, let cool, then store in the refrigerator in an airtight container with plastic wrap directly on the surface of the béchamel.

BLACK TRUFFLE & PROSCUITTO CROISSANTS

MAKES 4 SANDWICHES

This is a quick but luxurious sandwich that tastes much more complex than it is.

INGREDIENT	WEIGHT	VOLUME
4 fresh or day-old croissants	--------	--------
black truffle butter *(see Sources, page 250)*	25 grams	5 teaspoons per sandwich
Fromage d'Affinois Cheese with black truffle	available in 7.5-ounce rounds	2 to 3 slices per sandwich
sliced prosciutto	1 to 2 ounces	1 to 2 slices per sandwich
fresh arugula	2 ounces	a few leaves per sandwich

Preheat the oven to 350°F.

Slice the croissants in half lengthwise and spread both sides generously with the truffle butter.

Add 2 to 3 slices of the cheese to the base followed by slices of prosciutto and a generous handful of arugula.

Add the tops of the croissants, press down firmly, and warm in the oven for 5 minutes.

PAIN AUX NOISETTES

MAKES 20 PASTRIES

I really love this take on a classic pain au raisin, which when done correctly is one of my favorites. This rendition has just about everything: flaky pastry, creamy filling, and a crunchy, nutty flavor and texture. The recipe calls for five different kinds of nuts, but you can use less or more of any of them—have fun experimenting.

Roll the laminated croissant dough into a 30 by 20-inch rectangle that's around 1/5 inch (1/2 centimeter) thick.

Leaving a 1/2-inch border on each side, spread the pistachio cream over the dough in a thin layer, approximately 1 millimeter thick. Liberally sprinkle with the assorted nuts until all of the pastry cream is covered. With the palm of your hand, gently press the nuts into the dough, so they will not all end up in the middle of the dough when you begin to roll it.

Starting from the long end, tuck the first 1/2 inch of plain dough onto itself, make sure the seal is tight, and then pulling back with every roll, begin to roll the dough up into a spiral or log shape.

When you get to the last strip of plain dough, using the base of your hand, press it onto the table so it flattens out. Roll all the way to the end and then make a seam to complete the log.

With a serrated knife, slice the log crosswise into 20 pieces, around 3/4 inch thick, using long strokes so the dough is not crushed. Arrange the pieces of dough on a half-sheet pan lined with parchment paper, spiral side up, tucking the tail (the loose end that you just flattened out) underneath each spiral.

Cover with plastic wrap, and leave to proof somewhere warm for about 1 hour, or until the spirals have increased by one-third in size.

Preheat the oven to 350°F (if you have a convection oven, set it on medium fan), remove the plastic wrap, and bake for 13 to 15 minutes, until the pain aux noisettes are a deep golden-brown color all over. Leave them on the pan to cool on top of a wire rack.

INGREDIENT	WEIGHT	VOLUME
1 recipe laminated Croissant Dough (page 32)	--------	--------
1 recipe Pistachio Pastry Cream (page 47)	400 grams	--------
chopped hazelnuts	75 grams	10 tablespoons
chopped pistachios	75 grams	10 tablespoons
chopped pecans	75 grams	10 tablespoons
chopped cashews	75 grams	10 tablespoons
chopped almonds	75 grams	10 tablespoons

TIP: This is done so that the spirals will not unfurl during baking.

KOUIGN-AMANN: THE CROISSANT'S FAVORITE COUSIN

Kouign-amann (pronounced queen-aman) is a Breton cake containing layers of butter and sugar folded in, similar to puff pastry, albeit with fewer layers. The kouign-amann is a speciality of the town of Douarnenez in Finistère, Brittany, where it was first created in around 1860. The original recipe requires a ratio of 40 percent dough, 30 percent butter, and 30 percent sugar.

The recipes that follow further demonstrate the versatility of croissant dough, revealing how just a slightly different technique or an addition of a single ingredient can give you a completely different pastry. To prepare the kouign-amann (and variations on it), I use the same laminated dough, except on the last turn you dust the dough with sugar and then you bake the cakes in a muffin tin. The cake is slowly baked until the butter puffs up the dough and the sugar caramelizes. The result? Crunchy, rich, serving-sized cakes that feature a range of creative flavor pairings—from gianduja (hazelnut-chocolate) to lemon and poppy seed to a luscious Sicilian pastry cream filling. They're perfect for the morning, but you can eat them any time of the day. As always, I've tried to balance the sweetness of these recipes by including either a savory ingredient or something tart or sour, but the possibilities are endless—enjoy experimenting!

KOUIGN-AMANN

MAKES 12 TO 14 INDIVIDUAL SERVING-SIZED CAKES

Here's my take on the classic. Follow the instructions with care and you'll be rewarded with a muffin tin full of perfectly caramelized, decadently buttery pastries. These are versatile cakes that are delicious plain or will work with just about any filling, so enjoy exploring some different possibilities.

POOLISH STARTER

INGREDIENT	WEIGHT	VOLUME
all-purpose flour, preferably King Arthur Sir Galahad artisan flour	100 grams	13 tablespoons
instant yeast, SAF gold label	0.2 gram	1 pinch
water at 75°F	100 grams	7 tablespoons

In a bowl, combine the flour and yeast and mix them with your fingers until well combined. Gradually pour in the water and continue to mix with your fingers until there are no lumps.

Cover the bowl loosely with plastic wrap and let it sit at room temperature for 12 to 15 hours. The mixture should bubble when it's ready. (See tip, page 32.)

BUTTER BLOCK

INGREDIENT	WEIGHT	VOLUME
unsalted European-style butter	500 grams	2 1/4 cups

Spread out a piece of parchment paper on a work surface and then place the butter in the center. Top with a second piece of paper and, using a rolling pin, pound the butter as evenly as possible—the end result should be an even rectangle approximately 6 3/4 by 7 1/2 inches. Rotate the butter block 90 degrees and continue pounding with the rolling pin until this rectangle shape is achieved. Wrap in the parchment paper and store in the refrigerator. (See photos, page 34.)

KOUIGN-AMANN DOUGH

INGREDIENT	WEIGHT	VOLUME
bread flour, preferably King Arthur Special Patent	635 grams	4 cups + 14 tablespoons
sugar	15 grams	1 1/4 tablespoons
instant yeast, SAF gold label	6 grams	1 3/4 teaspoons
water, at room temperature	380 grams	1 1/2 cups
poolish starter (recipe above)	95 grams	scant 1 cup
unsalted European-style butter, at room temperature	20 grams	scant 1 1/2 tablespoons
salt	15 grams	2 1/4 teaspoons
superfine sugar, for finishing	-------	-------

Combine the flour, sugar, and yeast in the bowl of a stand mixer fitted with a dough hook and give it a quick mix to combine. Add the poolish, all but 50 grams (3 1/2 tablespoons) of the water, and the butter and mix on a low speed for 2 minutes. Scrape the bottom of the bowl with a spatula to make sure all the flour is combined.

Sprinkle the salt on top of the dough and continue to mix for 2 minutes; if the dough is looking dry at this point, add the reserved water. Mix on low speed for another 20 minutes, until the dough is smooth and has come cleanly away from the side of the bowl.

TIP: Mix this dough for a long time so the gluten strands develop and are strong—this will then allow you to stretch and roll out the dough and shape the kouign-amann.

Using a bench knife, scrape the dough out onto a lightly floured surface. Imagine that you are folding a letter to put in an envelope. Take the left side of the dough, stretch it, and bring it into the center of the dough, then stretch and fold the right side over to the opposite side. Repeat this process, this time working from the bottom and then the top.

Turn the dough over and place it on a lightly floured half-sheet pan. Cover with plastic wrap and let rest for 1 hour at room temperature.

Line a half-sheet pan with parchment paper. Carefully place the dough onto a lightly floured work surface. Without stretching the dough, gently but firmly pat the dough into a 10 by 8-inch rectangle using a rolling pin. Transfer to the prepared half-sheet pan and place in the freezer for 20 minutes.

BUTTER
LOCK-IN

Turn the dough out onto a lightly floured work surface and lightly flour the top. Using a rolling pin, roll the dough outward from its center, rotating and flipping it frequently and adding just enough flour to keep it from sticking. Your goal is to create a 16 by 8 by 1/2-inch rectangle.

Place the cold butter block directly in the middle of the rectangle. Fold each side of the dough into the center and pinch them together, so you cannot see any of the butter from above.

Using a rolling pin, press down firmly on the dough across the seam, rolling from one side to another. Then turn the dough 90 degrees so the short side faces you, and this time roll away from you. Continue to flip and rotate the dough, adding flour as necessary to keep it from sticking to the table, until you have a 22 by 9 by 3/8-inch rectangle.

Fold the bottom third of the dough up as if you were folding a letter, fold the top third down to cover the bottom third, then turn the block 90 degrees as if it were a book, with the opening on the right. This completes the first turn: Mark it by making a thumbprint in the dough, return the dough to the pan, cover it with plastic, and put it in the freezer for 20 minutes.

Repeat this process two more times, for a total of three turns.

TIP: Note that this dough is kept cold throughout; however, if the butter block starts to crack, or the dough does not roll smoothly, it means the temperature is too cold; give the dough a few minutes to soften before resuming.

FINISH THE
DOUGH

Remove the dough from the freezer and place it on a lightly floured surface with the opening on the right.

Roll the dough out until you have a 24 by 9-inch rectangle. Cut the dough crosswise to make two 12 by 9-inch rectangles.

Stack the two rectangles on top of each other and freeze for 20 minutes, or until the dough is firm again. The dough is now ready.

ASSEMBLE THE
KOUIGN-AMANN

Using softened butter and a pastry brush, liberally brush twelve to fourteen 4-inch muffin tins with the butter followed by sugar to coat; tap out any excess.

Lightly dust your work surface with superfine sugar. Remove one piece of the laminated dough from the freezer. Sprinkle a thin layer of sugar over the top and, with a short end toward you, roll the dough into a rectangle that's approximately 19 by 9 inches.

TIP: Work quickly when rolling dough topped with sugar, as the sugar will immediately start reacting with the moisture of the dough. Make sure you have everything you need ready to go before starting, otherwise it can quickly turn into a sugary mess.

Turn the dough so a long side is facing you and trim it so it's 18 inches long. Trim the other three edges so they are straight. (You can put the trimmings in a resealable plastic bag and reserve in the freezer.)

Cut out 5-inch squares from the dough. You are ready to begin shaping the kouign-amann.

Working with one square of dough at a time, take the opposite corners into the middle and press down with your forefinger, then repeat with the other two corners. Pick the dough up from the bottom, gently place it in a muffin tin, and push down in the middle; it should look almost like a flower. Repeat with the remaining squares of dough.

Cover with a cardboard or plastic box and allow to proof somewhere warm for about 2 hours.

Preheat the oven to 350°F.

Before baking, push the center of each piece of dough in one more time, just to prevent them from opening up during baking. Bake for 25 to 30 minutes, checking after 15 minutes. If they have opened up, just push them back down in the center, and if they are getting too dark, reduce the oven temperature to 325°F, but in that case give them an extra 10 minutes of baking time.

When a deep golden color has been achieved, remove the cakes from the oven, and immediately turn them out onto a wire rack. Allow them to cool upside-down, so the caramelized sugar sets before you touch it.

TIP: Be careful when taking the kouign-amanns out of the oven and turning them out of the pan; their tops are coated in molten sugar, so be sure you use oven mitts. But don't delay removing them from the pan; if you don't turn them out as soon as they come out of the oven, the sugar will set in the tins and you won't be able to remove them.

KOUIGN-AMANN

1 Brush a 4-inch muffin tin with softened butter

2 Coat each cavity with sugar, then tap out any excess

3 Cut the prepared laminated dough *(see page 32)* into 5-inch squares

4 On a lightly floured surface, take each square and bring its opposite corners into the middle of the dough

5 Bring the remaining corners into the middle of the dough to create a "parcel"

6 Place into prepared muffin tins

7 Using your finger push down the middle of the dough into the center of the tin

8 Bake for 18 to 20 minutes at 350°F, until a deep golden brown. Eat as is or choose a filling to pipe into the middle

DULCE DE LECHE KOUIGN-AMANN

MAKES 12 TO 14 SINGLE-SERVING CAKES

This is a Latin-inspired version of the kouign-amann. To prepare the thick, caramel-like filling, you simply simmer cans of sweetened condensed milk in water for a couple of hours.

INGREDIENT	WEIGHT	VOLUME
3 (14-ounce) cans sweetened condensed milk	--------	--------
1 recipe Kouign-Amann (page 58)	--------	--------
smoked Maldon sea salt, for finishing	--------	--------

Remove the labels from the cans of condensed milk, place the cans in a large deep saucepan, and cover them with water. Simmer over a low heat for 2 hours, checking to make sure the cans are covered with water during the entire time.

Using tongs, carefully remove the cans from the water and allow them to cool on a wire rack. The contents will be very hot: Do not try and open the cans until they are completely cool.

Once cooled, scoop out the contents of the cans (the dulce de leche) into a piping bag and fill the inside of the kouign-amanns. Sprinkle the tops with smoked salt.

BLACK SESAME KOUIGN-AMANN

MAKES 12 TO 14 SERVING-SIZED CAKES

This is one of my favorite variations on this classic cake: the savoriness of the sesame pairs beautifully with the sweetness of the kouign-amann. The perfect option for anyone who doesn't like anything too sweet in the morning.

INGREDIENT	WEIGHT	VOLUME
1 recipe Kougin-Amann dough (page 58), prepared through finishing	--------	--------
Black Sesame Sugar		
black sesame seeds	50 grams	1/3 cup
sugar	250 grams	1 1/4 cups

Make the black sesame sugar: In a dry skillet over medium-high heat, toast the seeds until they smoke.

Pulse the toasted seeds in a food processor with a blade attachment until they're mostly powder. Place them in a bowl with the sugar and stir until homogenous.

Assemble the kougin-amann as described on page 59, except replace the superfine sugar with black sesame sugar. Bake and cool as instructed.

LEMON & POPPY SEED KOUIGN-AMANN

MAKES 12 TO 14 SERVING-SIZED CAKES

This is another of my personal favorites. The poppy seeds give the pastry a savory note and the tart lemon curd cuts through the sweetness while still contributing a richness. Delicious and can be enjoyed at any time of day.

INGREDIENT	WEIGHT	VOLUME
1 recipe Kougin-Amann (page 58), prepared through finishing	--------	--------
Lemon Curd		
1 1/2 sheets gelatin	3 grams	--------
5 large eggs	250 grams	1 cup
sugar	225 grams	1 1/5 cups
zest and juice of 4 lemons	--------	--------
unsalted European-style butter	375 grams	1 2/3 cups

Soak the gelatin in cold water until soft; drain and squeeze out excess water.

In a saucepan over medium-high heat, combine the eggs, sugar, and lemon zest and juice, whisking constantly until the mixture comes to a boil.

Remove from the heat and whisk in the drained gelatin. Add the butter and whisk until incorporated.

Transfer to the bowl of a stand mixer with the whisk attachment and whisk until smooth and a slightly lighter yellow.

Allow to cool down and then reserve in a piping bag.

POPPY SEED SUGAR

INGREDIENT	WEIGHT	VOLUME
sugar	100 grams	1/2 cup
blue poppy seeds	100 grams	3/4 cup

Mix the sugar with the poppy seeds until evenly distributed.

Assemble the kougin-amann as described on page 59, except replace the superfine sugar with poppy seed sugar. Bake and cool as instructed.

Place the tip of the piping bag filled with lemon curd into the cavity of a kouign-amann and press until the lemon curd reaches the top. Repeat with the remaining cakes and lemon curd.

GIANDUJA KOUIGN-AMANN

MAKES 12 TO 14 SERVING-SIZED CAKES

Gianduja is a hazelnut-chocolate spread, originally from Italy, comprised of hazelnut paste and milk chocolate. The higher-grade pastes will have a higher percentage of hazelnuts and less oil (and a bigger price tag), but they will be more savory than sweet. Although it's not vital, for this recipe, I suggest a high-quality gianduja.

TIP: In this book, I suggest using Valrhona pistoles as they are easy to weigh, melt, and use; however, if you use a chocolate block instead, you will need to chop it up into small pieces so they melt evenly.

INGREDIENT	WEIGHT	VOLUME
1 recipe Kouign-Amann (page 58)	-------	-------
Gianduja Pastry Cream		
milk	270 grams	1 cup + 2 tablespoons
sugar	55 grams	4 1/2 tablespoons
3 1/4 large egg yolks	60 grams	3 tablespoons + 2 teaspoons
cornstarch	20 grams	2 1/2 tablespoons
salt	3.5 grams	1/2 teaspoon
unsalted European-style butter	35 grams	2 tablespoons + 1 teaspoon
hazelnut milk chocolate, ideally Valrhona Azélia pistoles (see Sources, page 250)	130 grams	3/4 cup chopped *(if using a chocolate block or bars instead)*

In a saucepan, whisk together the milk and half of the sugar and bring to a boil. In a bowl, whisk together the yolks, cornstarch, salt, and remaining sugar.

When the milk boils, slowly pour it over the egg mixture, whisking continually, then return it to the pot. Whisk over medium heat until the custard comes to a boil.

Remove the pot from the heat and add the butter and chocolate, whisking until fully incorporated, or use a hand blender for mixing if you have one. Cover with plastic wrap and allow to cool in the refrigerator.

CARAMELIZED HAZELNUTS

INGREDIENT	WEIGHT	VOLUME
sugar	250 grams	1 1/4 cups
water	125 grams	generous 1/2 cup
hazelnuts, whole, shelled	500 grams	3 1/2 cups
unsalted European-style butter	12 grams	2 1/2 teaspoons

In a pot over a medium heat, bring the sugar and water to 121°F; if you don't have a thermometer, this is the point when all the bubbles become small.

Add the hazelnuts to the sugar syrup and stir over medium-high heat using a candy spoon. The nuts will turn white as the sugar crystallizes and then the sugar will caramelize. When the nuts are evenly coated in an amber caramel, stir in the butter.

Spread the caramelized hazelnuts out on a silicone mat–lined half-sheet pan and allow to cool completely. Transfer to a resealable plastic bag and smash into chunks with a rolling pin.

When you're ready to assemble the kouign-amanns, fill a piping bag with the gianduja pastry cream. Place the tip into the cavity of a kouign-amann and fill it until the cream reaches the top. Repeat with the remaining cakes and pastry cream. Sprinkle with the caramelized hazelnuts and serve.

PB & J
KOUIGN-AMANN

MAKES 12 TO 14 SINGLE-SERVING CAKES

Bursting with Concord grape jam and crowned with a peanut butter glaze and chopped peanuts, this variation is perfect for kids—or the big kid in each of us.

INGREDIENT	WEIGHT	VOLUME
1 recipe Kouign-Amann (page 58)	--------	--------
1 recipe Concord Grape Jam (see opposite)	--------	--------
roasted unsalted peanuts, chopped	100 grams	3/4 cup
Peanut Butter Glaze		
creamy organic peanut butter	100 grams	6 tablespoons
neutral glaze (see Sources, page 250)	100 grams	1/3 cup
water	100 grams	7 tablespoons

Make the peanut butter glaze: In a saucepan, bring the peanut butter, neutral glaze, and water to a boil, whisking until smooth. Keep hot.

Fill a piping bag with the jam. Place the tip into the cavity of a kouign-amann and fill it until the jam reaches the top. Repeat with the remaining cakes and jam.

While the glaze is still hot, dip the top of each cake into the glaze, tapping off any excess. Immediately sprinkle with chopped peanuts and serve.

CONCORD GRAPE
KOUIGN-AMANN

MAKES 12 TO 14 SINGLE-SERVING CAKES

Concord grapes are native to New York City, but their seasons seem to be getting shorter and shorter—so if you can get them grab them. The smell of these grapes cooking away on the stovetop in your kitchen is something you will treasure. If you can't get ahold of the Concord variety, fresh or puréed black currants would be a good replacement.

INGREDIENT	WEIGHT	VOLUME
1 recipe Kouign-Amann (page 58)	--------	--------
Concord Grape Jam		
Concord grapes	5 pounds	--------

To make the jam, wash the grapes and then, using your thumb and forefinger, squeeze the flesh out of the skins, keeping the skins and flesh separate. The flesh will contain a lot of seeds.

Put the flesh and the seeds in a large pot and gradually bring to a boil. Boil for about an hour; the seeds should rise to the top.

Strain through a fine-mesh sieve, pushing the flesh through using the back of a spoon and leaving the seeds. Discard the seeds.

Put the skins in a bowl and pour the grape liquid over the skins. In a large pot, gradually bring the grape mixture to a boil, then cook for 10 minutes. Transfer to a food processor and blend until smooth, then pass the jam through a fine-mesh sieve again and let cool.

TIP: If the jam is a little loose, return to the heat and slowly cook it down until a thicker consistency has been achieved.

When cool, fill a piping bag with the jam. Place the tip into the cavity of a kouign-amann and fill it until the jam reaches the top. Repeat with the remaining cakes and jam and serve.

STRAWBERRIES & CREAM KOUIGN-AMANN

MAKES 12 TO 14 SINGLE-SERVING CAKES

These kouign-amanns, which feature local summer strawberries and clotted cream, are like a British picnic all rolled into one delicious cake. Clotted cream is made by indirectly heating full-cream cow's milk and leaving it to cool, allowing the cream to rise to the top and clot. A staple in the U.K., especially in the southwest of England, it has a nutty, cooked-milk flavor, which goes perfectly with strawberries.

INGREDIENT	WEIGHT	VOLUME
1 recipe Kouign-Amann (page 58)	--------	--------
1 jar clotted cream	about 250 grams	about 8 1/2 fluid ounces
1 punnet local strawberries, preferably organic	about 250 grams	about 20 strawberries, hulled and cut in half or sliced

Simply scoop the clotted cream into a piping bag and fill the inside of each kouign-amann by putting the tip of the piping bag into the cavity of the cake and pressing until the cream reaches the top. Place a couple of the freshly cut strawberries on top of the cream and try your best to share.

BRUNCH

Bread still fascinates me. Four ingredients but hundreds of possibilities. Flour. Yeast. Salt. Water. It amazes me how versatile these four basic ingredients can be; through small changes you can create a completely different bread, whether that's more time proofing or in the oven or one additional ingredient. And once you've made bread from scratch, you'll find that it's very hard to go back to store-bought loaves. All of the recipes in this section require mixing by hand and a bit of time to ferment and proof, but you'll see that the effort and the wait only adds to your satisfaction with the end result. Use these recipes as guidelines and then, when you've mastered them, feel free to experiment with your own flavors and additions.

In this chapter, I use the same basic dough to create four distinctive breads: ciabatta, focaccia, pizza bianca, and sourdough. These breads, in turn, can be used to create an assortment of brunch-worthy dishes that can be served as a light dinner or cocktail party bites as well. Instead of the usual quiche or tart, delight your Sunday morning guests with a slice of pizza bianca topped with wild mushrooms, duck confit, and duck eggs—or offer it in the afternoon with cocktails. Serve up the Coronation Chicken Salad on homemade sourdough for a repast that's fit for the Queen—or top that same bread with a housemade pastrami with cornichons and caramelized onions for a deli meal at home.

Prefer to wake up to something sweet? I open the chapter with recipes for some brunch-time favorites: lemony ricotta pancakes and doughnuts (fill them with jam, hazelnut chocolate spread, or a passion fruit curd—or make all three).

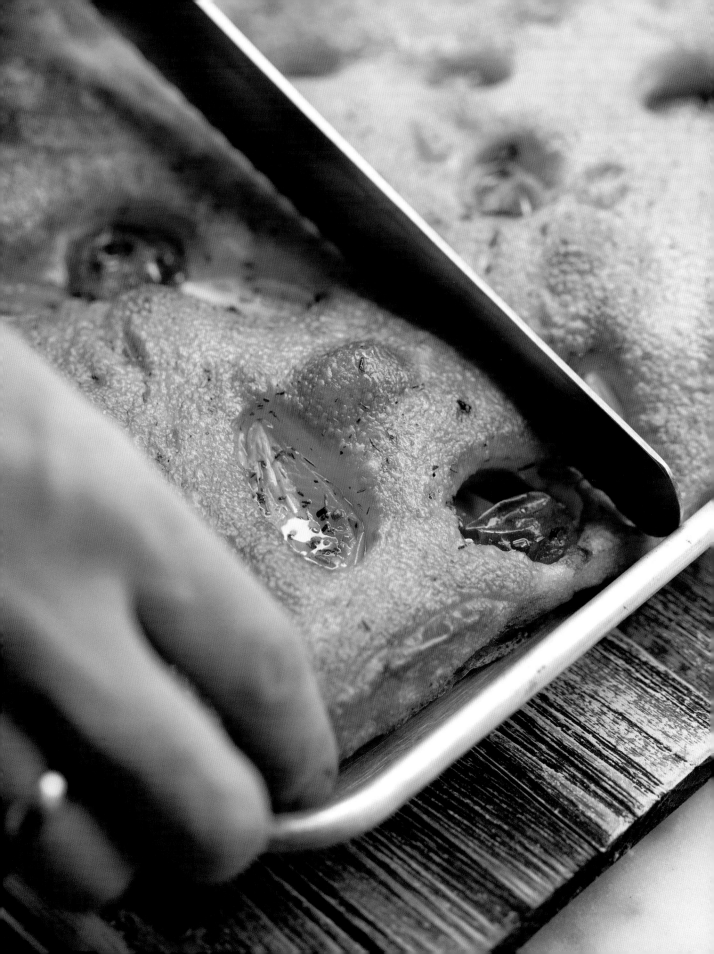

LEMON-RICOTTA PANCAKES

MAKES 16 SILVER DOLLAR-SIZED PANCAKES

My ideal Sunday breakfast, these are not as heavy as the classic American pancakes—the ricotta cheese and the lemon really lighten them up. They pair perfectly with my huckleberry compote, but if huckleberries are not readily available, fresh blueberries will make a great substitute.

INGREDIENT	WEIGHT	VOLUME
whole-milk ricotta cheese	900 grams or 32 ounces	3 3/4 cups
1 large egg	50 grams	3 tablespoons + 1/2 teaspoon
zest of 2 lemons	--------	--------
sugar	170 grams	14 tablespoons
all-purpose flour, preferably King Arthur Sir Galahad artisan flour	190 grams	1 cup + 9 tablespoons
baking powder	--------	1/2 teaspoon
pure vanilla extract (optional)	--------	1 teaspoon
vegetable oil, for frying	--------	2 to 3 tablespoons
1 recipe Huckleberry Compote (see right)	--------	--------

In a stand mixer with a beater attachment, mix the ricotta with the egg until smooth. Add the lemon zest and sugar and continue to mix on a low speed. Turn down the speed and gradually add the flour in three stages, then the baking powder and vanilla, if using, but be careful not to overmix.

Place the dough on a lightly floured work surface. Using a rolling pin, roll it out until about 1/2 inch thick.

Using a 4-inch ring cutter, punch out pancakes. Transfer to a half-sheet pan and allow them to rest in the refrigerator for at least 1 hour and up to 3 hours.

TIP: Any trimmings can be hand-rolled back into a ball, rerolled, and cut.

Heat the oil in a frying pan or skillet over medium heat. When the oil starts to shimmer, add the pancakes, working in batches to avoid crowding the pan. Cook for 3 to 4 minutes on each side until a deep golden-brown color has been achieved. Repeat with the remaining pancakes. Eat immediately with the huckleberry compote.

HUCKLEBERRY COMPOTE

INGREDIENT	WEIGHT	VOLUME
water	50 grams	3 tablespoons + 1 teaspoon
sugar	200 grams	1 cup
juice of 1/2 lemon	--------	--------
frozen huckleberries	500 grams	generous 3 1/2 cups

In a small saucepan, bring the water, sugar, and lemon juice to a boil. When the mixture turns into a clear syrup and develops small bubbles, add the huckleberries. Cook for 15 to 20 minutes, until the compote has thickened slightly. Either use immediately or allow to cool to room temperature and store in an airtight container in the refrigerator; use within three days or freeze for up to a month.

JAMMY DOUGHNUTS

MAKES 20 DOUGHNUTS

I am a big fan of doughnuts. Nowadays, it's possible to obtain a mind-blowing range of flavors, some enticing, some not so much, but the variety does show the versatility of a relatively basic recipe. Feel free to fill these doughnuts with gianduja (hazelnut chocolate spread) or the passionfruit curd recipe provided on the opposite page. However, it's hard to beat the taste of fried dough coated in sugar and filled with strawberry jam. So go ahead and make some Jammy Doughnuts, and enjoy!

In a medium bowl, whisk together the yeast, milk, water, and sugar to activate the yeast. In a stand mixer with a dough hook attachment, combine the flour, salt, and yeast mixture and mix on a medium speed for 10 minutes, until the dough has come together and there are no lumps. Gradually add the eggs, one at a time, incorporate fully before adding more, then gradually mix in the rum. Mix on a high speed for another 10 minutes, until the dough begins to come away from the sides of the bowl.

Gradually add the butter on a high speed, mixing until fully incorporated. Continue to mix for another 10 minutes, until the dough is glossy and comes away from the sides of the bowl cleanly.

Spray a large bowl with nonstick cooking spray, transfer the dough to the bowl, cover it with plastic wrap, and let sit in a warm place until it doubles in volume.

Once proofed, place the dough on a lightly floured work surface, and knock the dough back, folding the dough in on itself until the dough has lost some of its volume. Roughly roll it into a log shape.

Using a bench knife, cut the dough into twenty 50-gram pieces. Working with one piece of dough at a time, shape the doughnuts. Using the palm of your hand, press down on the dough while rotating your hand clockwise in a circular motion. You should end up with a perfectly round ball. Repeat with the remaining pieces of dough.

Line a half-sheet pan with parchment paper and spray the parchment with nonstick cooking spray. Transfer the balls of dough to the parchment, keeping space between them. Cover loosely with plastic wrap and allow to proof for another hour.

TIP: At this stage you could put the dough in the fridge and use it the next day, if you like. Just allow the dough to proof for another hour before you fry them.

Meanwhile, fill a large heavy-bottomed pot halfway with vegetable oil. Put the pot over a low to medium heat and gradually heat the oil until it reaches 375°F. If you don't have a thermometer, use small pieces of bread to test the temperature; if it begins to bubble as soon as you add the bread, the oil is ready.

TIP: Be very careful when heating a large amount of oil. Avoid splattering any water in the hot oil and never heat oil on a high heat—the oil will increase in temperature very quickly and become dangerous; low and slow is best.

Using a heatproof utensil, place 2 or 3 doughnuts at a time into the hot oil, turning them immediately so the dough is sealed by the oil. Fry them until a deep color has been achieved on all sides and there are no more bubbles on the side. Drain on paper towels and then roll the hot doughnuts in a plate of sugar. Repeat with the remaining balls of dough.

TIP: Coat the doughnuts in sugar while they are still hot so the sugar sticks and stays.

Fill a piping bag with strawberry jam. When the doughnuts are still hot, but cool enough to handle, using a paring knife, make a small incision in one of the doughnuts, insert the tip of the piping bag, and fill the doughnut with strawberry jam. Repeat with the remaining doughnuts.

Enjoy hot, sharing optional.

INGREDIENT	WEIGHT	VOLUME
fresh yeast	60 grams	8 1/2 teaspoons
(see Sources, page 251)		
milk	175 grams	11 1/2 tablespoons
water	30 grams	2 tablespoons
sugar, plus more for coating	100 grams	1/2 cup
the doughnuts		
all-purpose flour, preferably	1 kilogram	8 1/4 cups
King Arthur brand		
salt	20 grams	3 teaspoons
6 large eggs	300 grams	1 cup
		+ 3 tablespoons
dark rum	30 grams	2 tablespoons
unsalted European-style	200 grams	14 tablespoons
butter, softened		
vegetable oil, for frying	--------	--------
strawberry jam or	--------	--------
Concord Grape jam *(page 71)*,		
for filling doughnuts		

PASSIONFRUIT CURD
MAKES ABOUT 6 CUPS

Try this as a filling for your doughnuts: The passionfruit contributes an exotic tart taste that pairs really well with the sugary fried dough.

INGREDIENT	WEIGHT	VOLUME
6 large eggs	300 grams	1 cup +
		3 tablespoons
sugar	300 grams	1 1/2 cups
passionfruit juice	255 grams	1 cup
cold unsalted European-style	450 grams	2 cups
butter, cut into cubes		

In a large metal bowl, whisk the eggs, sugar, and juice together. Place the bowl over a saucepan of simmering water and whisk over medium heat until a mayonnaise consistency is achieved; do not stop whisking.

Allow to cool slightly, then beat in the diced butter. Allow to cool completely in the refrigerator before using.

SOURDOUGH BREAD

MAKES 2 LARGE LOAVES

A daily staple in France, this bread takes a little planning, but if you can work it into your schedule the effort is well worth it. Flavorful and versatile, this sourdough can be used for a couple of days if stored correctly, in a sealed paper bag or tightly wrapped in plastic wrap.

Make the starter: In a large bowl, mix the flour and the water together with your hand (the mixture will be loose). Cover tightly and leave in a warm place (ideally 60 to 70°F) to proof for 18 to 24 hours before using.

Make the dough: In a stand mixer with a bread hook, combine the starter, bread flour, rye flour, and all of the water. Mix on a low speed until the mixture resembles a shaggy mess. Add additional water, if necessary, 1 tablespoon at a time, while mixing, until the dough comes together to form a small ball. Stop the machine, cover the bowl with plastic wrap, and allow to proof for 1 hour.

After 1 hour, the dough will have risen slightly. Sprinkle the salt over the dough and finish mixing on a medium speed for 2 to 3 minutes.

Transfer the dough to a large bowl, cover with plastic wrap, and allow to proof for an additional 2 to 2 1/2 hours. After 1 hour, take the dough to a work surface and fold it once in half. Return to the bowl for the remaining proofing time.

Once the dough has doubled in size, remove it from the bowl and place it on a lightly floured work surface. Using a bench scraper, cut the dough in half. Using both hands, gently shape each piece into a round boule, or oblong loaf. Place each boule on a lightly floured half-sheet pan (one per pan), dust with additional flour, and score with a blade or small sharp knife in your preferred design. Allow to proof for another 2 hours, uncovered. Meanwhile, preheat your oven to 450°F.

When the final proof is complete, bake the boules for 35 to 45 minutes, until a deep golden color is achieved. Transfer to a cooling rack and allow to cool for a least 3 hours before cutting.

INGREDIENT	WEIGHT	VOLUME
Sour Starter		
bread flour, preferably King Arthur Special Patent (see Sources, page 250)	180 grams	1 cup + 6 tablespoons
water	235 grams	1 cup
Dough		
bread flour, preferably King Arthur Special Patent	500 grams	3 cups + 14 tablespoons
rye flour, preferably King Arthur brand	130 grams	generous 1 1/4 cups
water	580 grams	2 cups + 7 tablespoons
salt	17 grams	2 1/2 teaspoons

CIABATTA, FOCACCIA & PIZZA BIANCA STARTER DOUGH

The translation for the Italian name *ciabatta* is "slipper," as the shape of this loaf resembles a shoe. This bread was created in Italy as a response to the popularity of the French baguette. The secret with ciabatta is less is more; try to keep all the gas inside the bread by handling it as little as possible.

From this dough you can also make the focaccia and pizza bianca recipes that follow, so I encourage you to make a larger batch of the dough and divide it up. No special machinery is needed to make these recipes.

In a bowl, combine the flour and yeast and mix them with your fingers until well combined. Gradually pour in the water and continue to mix with your fingers until there are no lumps.

Cover the bowl loosely with plastic wrap and let it sit at room temperature for 12 to 15 hours. The mixture should bubble when it's ready.

POOLISH STARTER
FOR CIABATTA / FOCACCIA / PIZZA BIANCA

INGREDIENT	WEIGHT	VOLUME
all-purpose flour, preferably King Arthur Sir Galahad artisan flour	500 grams	4 cups + 2 tablespoons
instant yeast, SAF gold label	0.2 grams	1 pinch
water at 75°F	500 grams	2 cups + 2 tablespoons

CIABATTA, FOCACCIA & PIZZA BIANCA

One dough, three different breads. What could be more practical than that?

INGREDIENT	WEIGHT	VOLUME
all-purpose flour, preferably King Arthur Sir Galahad artisan flour	1 kilogram	8 1/4 cups
fresh yeast (see Sources, page 251)	15 grams	2 teaspoons
salt	30 grams	4 1/2 teaspoons
poolish starter (page 83)	700 grams	1/2 recipe
water	680 grams	2 cups + 14 tablespoons
cornmeal, for the pizza bianca	--------	--------
olive oil, for the foccacia	--------	--------

In a large bowl, mix together the flour, yeast, and salt. Make a large well in the middle of the flour mixture, add the starter, and then gradually add the water, mixing with your hand until combined.

TIP: At this stage, the dough will look like a wet, sticky mess. That's okay—this is a wet-style dough, which is why the bread will be light and airy once it's baked.

Cover the bowl with plastic wrap and leave somewhere warm for 2 to 3 hours, or more depending on your environment, until the dough doubles in size.

When the dough has doubled, heavily flour your work surface, carefully pour or gently pull the dough onto the table. (Remember, the idea with this dough is to keep all the gas in, so the less you handle it, the better.)

ASSEMBLE AND BAKE THE CIABATTA LOAVES
MAKES 15 SANDWICH LOAVES

Gently pat the base dough on your table into a rough rectangle shape. Using a bench knife, cut the dough into fifteen 150-gram pieces.

With both hands, gently roll the dough into rough round boules. Fold the boules in half and gently pull the ends of each boule to get a rough rectangle shape that's approximately 2 by 6 inches.

With the seam facing down, place the rectangle of dough on a half-sheet pan lined with parchment paper. Sprinkle the dough liberally with flour and allow to proof for another hour.

Preheat the oven to 500°F. (If you own baking tiles, place them on the middle rack of the oven.)

TIP: All of these breads bake much better if they have direct contact with baking tiles or a pizza stone. If you don't have either of these, a half-sheet pan is fine, but think about investing in these inexpensive additions to get that true Roman-style bread.

Place the bread in the oven and reduce the oven temperature to 450°F. Bake for 10 to 15 minutes, until a deep brown color has been achieved.

Let the loaves cool completely on a wire rack before you eat them.

ASSEMBLE AND BAKE
THE FOCCACIA
MAKES 2 LOAVES

Weigh out a 1.2-kilogram piece from the base dough (about half of the total dough) on your table.

Using your hand, liberally grease a half-sheet pan with olive oil. Place the dough on the pan and, using your fingers, spread out the dough, pushing it into the corners of the pan to create an even layer.

TIP: If the dough keeps pulling back from the corners, leave it for 10 minutes and try again; the gluten strands will relax and become easier to manage.

Using your fingertips, make little dents all over the dough, then liberally pour some more olive oil over the bread. Repeat with another 1.2 kilograms of dough. Allow to proof for another hour.

Preheat the oven to 400°F.

Place one pan of foccacia in the middle of the oven, on top of baking tiles if you have them. Close the door then reduce the oven temperature to 375°F.

Bake for 15 to 20 minutes, until a deep golden-brown color has been achieved. Return the oven temperature to 400°F to bake the second foccacia.

Let cool on the pan on a wire rack.

ASSEMBLE AND BAKE
THE PIZZA BIANCA
MAKES 3 PIZZAS

Divide the base dough on your table into three 400-gram pieces.

Preheat the oven to 500°F.

If you have a pizza stone, sprinkle it with cornmeal; if not, turn a half-sheet pan upside-down and do the same.

Place one piece of the dough on the stone or pan and, using your fingers, spread out the dough, pushing it to the corners and making it as even and flat as possible.

Place the pizza still on the stone or pan inside the oven and reduce the oven temperature to 450°F. Bake for 8 to 10 minutes, until a light color has been achieved. Repeat twice for the two remaining pieces of dough.

TIP: The idea behind pizza bianca is to bake it at a high temperature very quickly to achieve a light and soft bread. If you bake it for too long or let it get too much color, the pizza won't be soft. Instead, because the dough is so thin, the pizza will end up more like a cracker.

TOMATO & HERB FOUGASSE

MAKES 2 LOAVES

What's known as focaccia in Italy is fougasse in Provence. This yeasted flatbread is flecked with tomatoes (both fresh and sundried), fresh herbs, and Parmesan and finished with a drizzle of olive oil and an additional sprinkle of Parmesan. Traditionally it is shaped like a sheaf of wheat and served to celebrate the beginning of the harvest, but there is no need to limit this bread to just once a year.

Put the focaccia dough in a stand mixer with a dough hook and add the sun-dried and fresh tomatoes, the rosemary, thyme, and Parmesan, reserving some of the cheese to sprinkle on at the end. Mix for 10 minutes on speed 2 (or low speed), until all the ingredients are incorporated.

Transfer the dough to a larger bowl, cover with plastic wrap, and allow to proof in a warm place for 1 1/2 hours, or until doubled in size.

Turn the proofed dough out onto a lightly floured surface and knead it for 2 to 3 minutes using the base of your hand.

Grease a half-sheet pan with 2 to 3 tablespoons of olive oil, then place half of the dough on the pan and begin to flatten it out using your fingertips; the shape you are trying to achieve is an oval.

When you have created the oval shape, using a bench knife, make two 3-inch scores on each side of the oval and one score in the top-middle of the dough; the result should resemble a sheaf of wheat. Repeat with the remaining dough. Allow to proof for another hour.

When you're ready to bake, preheat the oven to 400°F.

Brush the proofed dough with olive oil, sprinkle with some sea salt and the reserved Parmesan, and bake for 15 minutes, or until lightly golden. Allow to cool on a wire rack until it reaches room temperature before serving.

INGREDIENT	WEIGHT	VOLUME
1 recipe focaccia dough (page 86)	--------	--------
minced sun-dried tomatoes (oil drained)	100 grams	1 cup
minced fresh tomatoes	200 grams	1 1/4 cups
minced fresh rosemary	2.5 grams	1/2 tablespoon
minced fresh thyme	2.5 grams	1 tablespoon
grated Parmesan	100 grams	1 cup
olive oil, for greasing and drizzling	--------	--------
sea salt to taste	--------	--------

TIP: You may need to allow the dough to rest during shaping, to allow the gluten strands to relax. If the dough keeps pulling back, leave it for 5 minutes and come back to it.

CHERRY, GOLDEN RAISIN, & WALNUT BREAD

MAKES 6 OR 7 SMALL LOAVES

This is one of my favorite breads. It's made from a more traditional type of dough than ciabatta, but as with the pizza bianca, many variations on it are possible. Because this version is studded with dried cherries, raisins, and walnuts, it goes especially well with cheese. A bonus is that this bread is actually better the next day.

INGREDIENT	WEIGHT	VOLUME
Starter		
fresh yeast	25 grams	3 1/2 teaspoons
(see Sources, page 251)		
water	400 grams	1 2/3 cups
all-purpose flour, preferably	680 grams	5 2/3 cups
King Arthur Sir Galahad		
artisan flour		
salt	5 grams	3/4 teaspoon
sugar	50 grams	1/4 cup
powdered milk	12 grams	1 tablespoon
		+ 1 1/2 teaspoons
unsalted European-style	150 grams	2/3 cup
butter, softened		

In a stand mixer with a dough hook, mix all the ingredients until they come together to form a ball. Place in an airtight container and allow to proof for 24 hours in the refrigerator before using.

INGREDIENT	WEIGHT	VOLUME
starter (recipe at left)	--------	--------
Dough		
fresh yeast	25 grams	3 1/2 teaspoons
water	425 grams	1 cup + 13 tablespoons
bread flour, preferably	750 grams	5 3/4 cups
King Arthur Special Patent		
rye flour, preferably	180 grams	1 3/4 cups
King Arthur brand		
sugar	75 grams	6 tablespoons
salt	15 grams	2 1/4 teaspoons
golden raisins	250 grams	1 3/4 cups
dried cherries	300 grams	generous 2 cups
chopped walnuts	250 grams	2 cups + 3 tablespoons

In the bowl of a stand mixer, add the previously made starter, fresh yeast, water, flours, sugar, salt, and dried fruit and nuts, attach a dough hook attachment, and mix on a low to medium speed for 2 minutes until the dough and starter come together to form a ball and come away from the side of the bowl cleanly. Increase the speed and mix for 7 additional minutes, which will help develop the gluten strands.

Remove from the bowl and divide evenly into six or seven 480-gram balls.

TIP: Don't be intimidated by the size of this recipe: this bread is great the next day and, if wrapped tightly in plastic wrap, the extra loaves can be frozen for up to three weeks.

On a lightly floured surface, gently knead each ball for 2 to 3 minutes, then shape each one into a short log. Allow to rest for 10 minutes and then repeat the process, gradually tapering both ends of the logs to create loaves. Allow to rest for another 10 minutes, then repeat this process until the loaves of dough are 8 to 10 inches long with points on each end.

Proof in a warm place, covered with clean kitchen towels, until the loaves have roughly doubled in size, which should take 1 to 1 1/2 hours. Preheat the oven to 400°F.

Place two of the proofed loaves on a half-sheet pan or baking tile and bake for about 20 minutes, until a deep brown color is achieved. Cool on a wire rack before slicing. Repeat with the remaining loaves.

BLACK TRUFFLE & SMOKED BLACK PEPPER BRIOCHE

MAKES SIX TO EIGHT 4 X 8-INCH LOAVES

This light yeast bread is rich with eggs and butter. In this recipe I have incorporated shaved truffle, truffle oil, and a smoky black pepper to take things up a notch.

In a stand mixer with a bread hook attachment, mix all of the ingredients except the butter on a low speed for 5 minutes. Add the butter and mix on high speed for 10 minutes, until the dough comes away from the sides of the bowl.

Remove the bowl from the mixer, cover with plastic wrap so it's touching the surface of the dough, and let rest in the refrigerator for 24 hours.

The next day, divide the dough into 6 to 8 pieces, shape into loaves, and place in greased 4 by 8-inch bread pans. Let rise until doubled in size.

Preheat the oven to 350°F. Bake for about 20 minutes, or until a deep golden-brown color is achieved. Allow to cool on a wire rack before slicing.

INGREDIENT	WEIGHT	VOLUME
bread flour, preferably King Arthur Special Patent	1 kilogram	7 3/4 cups
7 eggs	350 grams	1 cup + 6 tablespoons
salt	30 grams	4 1/2 teaspoons
sugar	200 grams	1 cup
fresh yeast	35 grams	5 teaspoons
milk	220 grams	14 1/2 tablespoons
black truffle shavings	200 grams/ 7 ounces	--------
truffle oil	30 grams	2 1/4 tablespoons
smoked black pepper *(see Sources, page 251)*	50 grams	7 1/4 tablespoons
cold unsalted European-style butter, cut into cubes	520 grams	2 1/3 cups

PIZZA BIANCA
SERVES 6

Pizza needs neither tomato sauce nor vast amounts of cheese to be incredibly satisfying, as this white (bianca) version demonstrates. It's a great alternative to sandwiches and the possibilities are endless. Here are some of my favorite variations.

HERB PIZZA BIANCA

INGREDIENT	WEIGHT	VOLUME
1 Pizza Bianca (page 86)	--------	--------
extra-virgin olive oil, for drizzling	--------	--------
Maldon sea salt, for sprinkling	--------	--------
chopped fresh rosemary, thyme, and sage	--------	3 tablespoons

Liberally drizzle the warm pizza bianca with the olive oil and generously sprinkle with sea salt. Scatter the mixed herbs on top.

PROSCUITTO, RICOTTA, & FIG PIZZA BIANCA

INGREDIENT	WEIGHT	VOLUME
fig jam	75 grams	1/3 cup
fresh ricotta cheese	100 grams	6 1/2 tablespoons
Maldon sea salt and freshly cracked pepper, for sprinkling	--------	--------
thinly sliced prosciutto	1 to 2 ounces	--------
arugula	1 to 2 ounces	--------

Spread the fig jam over the warm pizza bianca. Using a spatula, spread the fresh ricotta in patches over the pizza. Season with sea salt and black pepper. Loosely lay the proscuitto slices over the cheese. Generously cover the pizza with fresh arugula. If they are in season, you can also add fresh figs cut into quarters to finish.

TARTE FLAMBÉE
SERVES 6

This classic dish from the Alsace region of France is the perfect way to use up any leftover pizza bianca dough. Crème fraîche, caramelized onions, bacon lardons, and fresh thyme, baked on a thin-crust dough, come together to create a simple yet very satisfying meal.

INGREDIENT	WEIGHT	VOLUME
4 white onions	--------	--------
olive oil	--------	3 tablespoons
chopped fresh thyme	--------	2 tablespoons
salt and freshly ground black pepper to taste	--------	--------
10 slices smoked bacon	--------	--------
1/4 recipe Pizza Bianca Dough (page 86)	300 grams	--------
crème fraîche	150 grams	10 tablespoons

Preheat the oven to 375°F.

Peel and thinly slice the onions. Heat the olive oil in a large skillet over medium heat and add the onions, thyme, and salt to taste. Stir with a wooden spoon, then cover with a lid until the onions are completely soft, about 15 minutes. Remove the lid and continue to cook the onions until they begin to caramelize, stirring occasionally so they don't stick to the bottom of the pan or burn. When a deep caramelization is achieved, after about 15 minutes, taste and season with salt and pepper. Reserve.

Using kitchen scissors, cut the bacon crosswise into thin slices. In a non-stick frying pan, cook the bacon lardons until crisp, and then drain them on paper towels.

Grease a 20 by 40-inch half-sheet pan with additional olive oil. Place the pizza dough on the half-sheet pan and, using your hands, gently push the dough into the corners of the pan to create a thin sheet of dough.

Bake for 8 to 10 minutes, just until the dough is cooked but without too much color. Spread the crème fraîche over the pizza crust in a thin layer, then scatter the caramelized onions and bacon lardons on top.

Continue to bake for another 5 to 7 minutes, until the crème fraîche begins to bubble. Eat it hot, straight out of the oven.

WILD MUSHROOM, DUCK CONFIT & DUCK EGG PIZZA BIANCA

The earthiness of sautéed mushrooms combined with duck confit and a duck egg cracked over the top make for a flavorful and sophisticated take on pizza bianca. If you can't get a duck egg, a free-range chicken egg works perfectly well.

Preheat the oven to 400°F.

In a large sauté pan, heat the olive oil over high heat until it begins to ripple. Add the garlic cloves and thyme sprig, tossing to coat them in the oil. Add the mushrooms and continue to cook over high heat, stirring periodically, for about 10 minutes, until the mushrooms have softened. Deglaze the pan with the sherry vinegar. Season with salt and pepper, taste and adjust seasoning if necessary, then drain the mushrooms on paper towels, discarding the garlic and thyme.

Place the pizza bianca on a half-sheet pan lined with parchment paper. Spread the mushrooms over the pizza bianca to cover. Season again with salt and pepper. Scatter the shredded duck on top of the mushrooms. Crack the duck egg in the center of the pizza and immediately place it in the oven, reducing the oven temperature to 375°F.

Cook for 8 to 10 minutes, until the egg is cooked but the yolk is still runny. Season the egg with salt and pepper and enjoy the pizza immediately.

INGREDIENT	WEIGHT	VOLUME
olive oil	--------	3 tablespoons
2 cloves garlic	--------	--------
1 sprig thyme	--------	--------
wild mushrooms, cleaned, washed, and sliced	500 grams or generous 1 pound	--------
sherry vinegar	50 grams	generous 3 tablespoons
sea salt and freshly cracked black pepper to taste	--------	--------
duck confit, shredded (see Sources, page 250)	100 grams or 3 1/2 ounces	-------
1 duck egg	--------	--------
1 Pizza Bianca (page 86)	--------	--------

CAULIFLOWER, PARMESAN & JALAPEÑO FOCACCIA

This trio of ingredients comes together to create a focaccia with an unexpected kick. Cornmeal scattered over the top protects the cauliflower from burning and contributes a pleasing crunch.

Preheat the oven to 400°F.

Remove and discard the green stems from the cauliflower and cut the head into quarters. Using a mandoline with a guide, thinly slice the cauliflower and put it in a large bowl. Thinly slice the jalapeño and garlic with the mandoline and add them to the bowl.

TIP: Whenever you're using a mandoline, always use the guard so you don't lose the tip of a finger—it won't taste good in the pizza!

Toss the cheese into the bowl along with a generous splash of olive oil, season with sea salt and cracked pepper, and mix with your hands until the vegetables are well coated.

Using your hands again, scoop out the mixed vegetables and gently press them on top of the raw focaccia dough, making sure all the surface of the dough is covered. Sprinkle a light layer of cornmeal over the entire pizza.

Reduce the oven temperature to 350°F and bake for 20 to 25 minutes, until the focaccia is cooked through. Let cool on a wire rack before serving.

INGREDIENT	WEIGHT	VOLUME
1 head cauliflower	--------	--------
1 jalapeño chili	--------	--------
1 clove garlic	--------	--------
Parmesan cheese, grated	100 grams	1 1/3 cups
olive oil, for coating the vegetables	--------	--------
sea salt and freshly cracked pepper to taste	--------	--------
cornmeal, for sprinkling	--------	--------
1 half-sheet pan of Focaccia Dough *(page 87)*	--------	--------

GRILLED CHEESE ON SOURDOUGH
WITH BLACK TRUFFLE BUTTER AND PICKLED SHALLOTS
SERVES 4

Remember that amazing sourdough you made? Do it justice with this upscale take on grilled cheese.

INGREDIENT	WEIGHT	VOLUME
black truffle butter (see Sources, page 250)	--------	3 teaspoons per sandwich
8 thick slices Sourdough Bread (page 82)	--------	--------
aged cheddar cheese, such as Cabot clothbound cheddar	2 to 3 ounces	2 or 3 slices per sandwich
Pickled Shallots (see right)	--------	1 teaspoon per sandwich

Preheat the oven to 350°F.

Spread the truffle butter on every slice of bread. Place 2 or 3 slices of the cheddar on 4 slices of the bread followed by the pickled shallots. Place the other 4 slices of bread on top. Then spread truffle butter on both the tops and bottoms of the sandwiches.

Heat a nonstick pan over medium heat. Cook a sandwich on one side until golden brown, then flip it over and repeat on the other side. Repeat with the remaining sandwiches.

Arrange the sandwiches on a half-sheet pan and put them in the oven for 5 minutes to finish melting the cheese. Enjoy hot.

PICKLED SHALLOTS
MAKES ABOUT 2 CUPS

INGREDIENT	WEIGHT	VOLUME
red wine	--------	6 tablespoons
port	--------	6 tablespoons
crème de cassis	--------	3 tablespoons
1 bay leaf	--------	--------
1 sprig fresh thyme	--------	--------
1 clove garlic	--------	--------
5 shallots, thinly sliced	--------	--------

Combine all the ingredients except the shallots and bring to a boil.

Allow the brine to cool slightly, then pour it over shallots. Let cool, then store in an airtight container in the refrigerator.

CHARRED SPICED EGGPLANT SPREAD TOASTS
WITH POMEGRANATE SEEDS AND LEMON
MAKES 6 OPEN-FACED SANDWICHES

A smoky, silky eggplant dip garnished with a trio of Middle Eastern flavors makes for an irresistible bruschetta your guests won't soon forget.

Preheat the oven to 400°F.

Char the eggplants on all sides with a blowtorch or by placing them directly on a gas burner and rotating them until blackened on all sides. Wrap each eggplant in foil and bake for 40 minutes, or until the flesh is very tender.

Heat a small amount of olive oil in a large pot, add the garlic, and cook over medium heat until it begins to color slightly. Add the cumin, curry, and coriander and continue to cook until the seeds begin to pop. Add the onions and let them sweat until soft, then add the chopped tomatoes and cook until the mixture is dry. Season with salt and freshly ground black pepper.

Remove the eggplants from the foil and cut them in half. Spoon out the flesh, discarding the skin, and add the flesh to the onion mixture. Stir to combine, season again with salt and pepper to taste, and cook until dry. Allow to cool, then stir in the chopped cilantro and parsley. Taste for salt and pepper and adjust accordingly. (You can store the spread covered in the refrigerator, for 3 to 4 days before serving.)

Spread the eggplant dip on the toasted pizza bianca or focaccia and top with pomegranate seeds and lemon zest.

INGREDIENT	WEIGHT	VOLUME
8 to 10 medium-sized eggplants	--------	--------
olive oil, for cooking	--------	--------
4 cloves garlic, minced	--------	--------
cumin seeds	30 grams	5 tablespoons
curry powder	30 grams	5 tablespoons
coriander seeds	20 grams	4 tablespoons
4 onions, diced	--------	--------
1 (14-ounce) can diced tomatoes	--------	--------
salt to taste	--------	--------
pepper to taste	--------	--------
1 bunch fresh cilantro, leaves only, chopped	40 grams	--------
1 bunch fresh parsley, leaves only, chopped	40 grams	--------
6 slices Pizza Bianca or Focaccia (page 87), toasted	--------	--------
For Garnish		
pomegranate seeds, for sprinkling	--------	--------
zest of 1 lemon	--------	--------

MORNING PROVISIONS

TRI-COLORED MARKET RADISHES
WITH WHIPPED GOAT CHEESE AND SABLÉ BRETON
SERVES 6 TO 8

Here, a light tangy goat cheese spread and crispy radish slices top a sweet and salty shortbread crust.

On a lightly floured surface, begin rolling out the sablé Breton dough—we are aiming for a 12 by 12-inch square that's just 1/8 inch thick. Trim off any excess dough and reserve. Carefully transfer the square of dough to a half-sheet pan lined with parchment paper. Allow to rest in the refrigerator for at least 1 hour and up to 3 hours.

Meanwhile, preheat the oven to 350°F and make the whipped goat cheese filling: In a stand mixer fitted with a whisk attachment, begin to mix the goat cheese, cream, and half of the salt and pepper on low speed, then increase the speed and whip until smooth.

Remove the sablé Breton from the fridge, and using a fork, dock the dough evenly all over. Whisk up the remaining egg yolk from the sablé recipe and brush the top of the dough. Bake in the preheated oven on the middle rack for 10 to 12 minutes, until golden brown. Allow to cool on the half-sheet pan until the crust reaches room temperature. (Do not turn off the oven.)

Wash the radishes and remove the stems and tips. Using either a small sharp knife or a mandoline, thinly slice the radishes.

When the sablé is cool, spread the whipped goats' cheese evenly over the entire square. Arrange the radishes over the goat cheese, alternating their color and size and making sure each one overlaps the previous slice.

Using a pastry brush, brush the radish slices with the melted butter and sprinkle the remaining salt and pepper on top.

Bake again for 5 to 7 minutes until the radishes just begin to soften. Best enjoyed hot and fresh, straight from the oven.

INGREDIENT	WEIGHT	VOLUME
1 recipe Sablé Breton dough (see below)	--------	---------
goat cheese, without rind	250 grams or 8 3/4 ounces	--------
heavy cream	75 grams	1/3 cup
European-style butter, melted	100 grams	7 tablespoons
Maldon sea salt	10 grams	1 3/4 teaspoons
freshly ground black pepper	15 grams	1 1/2 tablespoons
1 bunch tri-colored radishes	--------	--------

SABLÉ BRETON DOUGH
MAKES ONE HALF-SHEET PAN

INGREDIENT	WEIGHT	VOLUME
salted European-style butter	200 grams	1/2 cup + 5 tablespoons
sugar	120 grams	1/2 cup + 1 tablespoon
3 egg yolks	60 grams	1/4 cup
vanilla extract	--------	1 tablespoon
all-purpose flour, preferably King Arthur Sir Galahad artisan flour	280 grams	2 cups + 2 tablespoons

In a stand mixer with a paddle attachment, beat the butter and sugar together for about 3 minutes, until light in color and fluffy.

Add two of the egg yolks and the vanilla extract and beat on a medium speed until incorporated. Stop the mixer and scrape down the sides of the bowl to the center, using a rubber spatula. Add the flour and mix on a low speed until the dough just comes together.

HOUSEMADE PASTRAMI
WITH CORNICHONS AND CARAMELIZED ONIONS
MAKES 8 SANDWICHES

Forget a trip to the deli—bring the deli home. Homemade pastrami, pickles, and caramelized onions, stacked tall on your own house-baked bread, is a guaranteed crowd pleaser. Serve this on freshly toasted ciabatta or focaccia.

First, make the pastrami brine: In a large heavy-bottomed pot, combine all the brine ingredients and bring to rapid boil over a high heat, then turn off the heat and allow to cool for 3 to 4 hours, until the brine is at room temperature.

To make the pastrami rub, combine all the ingredients in a food processor and blend together until you achieve a powder-like texture (it's not an issue if there are a few lumps). Store in a sealed airtight container until needed. It will last up to three months if stored properly.

Brine the brisket: Place the cooled brine liquid into a large plastic container, then place the whole piece of brisket inside, so it is totally submerged. Seal with a plastic lid or plastic wrap and store in the refrigerator for at least 3 days, ideally 5 days.

To finish the pastrami: Remove the brisket from the brine liquid and place on a half-sheet pan with a cooling rack. Using a paper towel, gently dab the brisket to dry it off slightly. Using your hands, rub the spice mix into the brisket, making sure all the meat is covered with a good layer of the spice mix. Leave to marinate for at least 2 hours or ideally overnight.

Meanwhile, preheat the oven to 325°F. Bake the brisket on the cooling rack and pan until it has an internal temperature of 160°F, 2 to 3 hours, depending on your oven. Remove from the oven and wrap in aluminum foil and allow to rest for 1 1/2 to 2 hours. Eat immediately (recommended) or store in the fridge for up to three days.

To make the caramelized onions, slice the onions thinly and cook down with the oil on a low heat until caramelized and season with salt and pepper.

Slice the brisket and serve on the ciabatta with cornichons and the caramelized onions.

INGREDIENT	WEIGHT	VOLUME
8 thick slices ciabatta or focaccia, toasted (page 83)		--------
1 piece beef brisket	about 4 pounds	--------
20 cornichons, sliced in half lengthways	--------	--------
Pastrami Brine		
water	3.785 kilograms	1 gallon
kosher salt	140 grams	1 cup
sugar	200 grams	1 cup
star anise	10 grams	2 tablespoons
pickling spice	10 grams	1 tablespoon
fennel seed	10 grams	1 tablespoon
cinnamon stick	10 grams	about 3 inches
4 bay leaves	--------	--------
coriander seeds	15 grams	1 1/2 tablespoons
2 cloves garlic	--------	--------
Pastrami Rub		
kosher salt	40 grams	1/4 cup
sweet paprika	45 grams	1/4 cup
hot paprika	10 grams	2 tablespoons
coriander seeds	60 grams	6 tablespoons
brown sugar	50 grams	1/4 cup packed
black peppercorns	60 grams	6 tablespoons
yellow mustard seeds	20 grams	2 tablespoons
10 cloves garlic, minced	--------	--------
red pepper flakes	5 grams	1/2 teaspoon
star anise	10 grams	2 tablespoons
fennel seeds	30 grams	3 tablespoons
Caramelized Onions		
6 onions	--------	--------
vegetable oil	--------	3 tablespoons

CORONATION CHICKEN SALAD
WITH CUCUMBER ON CIABATTA
MAKES 4 TO 6 SANDWICHES

This is a classic British sandwich filling: slightly curried chicken and mayonnaise with fresh and dried fruit, sliced almonds, and fresh herbs. I like to serve it on ciabatta rolls.

Rub the olive oil all over the chicken. Scatter the lemon zest over the top and season with salt and black pepper.

Arrange the chicken in a single layer in a steamer basket and steam over a pot of boiling water for 10 to 12 minutes, or until cooked through, then set aside to cool.

Melt the butter in a frying pan over medium heat. Add the shallots and chili pepper to the pan and fry them for 5 minutes. Stir in the curry powder and cook for 2 to 3 minutes. Stir in the tomato purée and cook for another minute. Pour in the wine and continue to cook for about 30 minutes more, until the volume of the liquid has reduced by half.

Stir in the jam with 2 cups (500 ml) of water and continue to simmer for about 20 minutes, until the volume of the liquid has reduced by half. Set aside to cool.

Mix the mayonnaise and the crème fraiche in a large bowl until well combined, then stir in the curry dressing in the saucepan. Fold in the mangoes, spring onions, reserved lemon juice, and the cilantro.

Cut the chicken into bite-sized pieces and fold them into the mayonnaise mixture. Season with salt, freshly ground black pepper, and Tabasco to taste. Serve on the ciabatta rolls, with sliced English cucumbers and toasted almond slivers. For an added touch, garnish with shiso leaves.

INGREDIENT	WEIGHT	VOLUME
olive oil, for coating the chicken	--------	--------
4 free-range boneless chicken breasts, skin removed	--------	--------
zest and juice of 3 lemons	--------	--------
sea salt and freshly ground black pepper to taste	--------	--------
knob of butter	50 grams	3 1/2 tablesoons
4 shallots, finely chopped	--------	--------
2 green chili peppers, deseeded and finely chopped	--------	--------
Madras curry powder	17 grams	8 teaspoons
tomato purée	30 grams	2 tablespoons
dry white wine	500 grams	2 cups + 4 teaspoons
apricot jam	100 grams	1/3 cup
mayonnaise	465 grams	2 cups + 2 tablespoons
crème fraîche	340 grams	1 1/4 cups
3 mangoes, peeled and pitted, flesh diced	--------	--------
10 spring onions, finely chopped	--------	--------
chopped fresh cilantro	30 grams	6 tablespoons
Tabasco sauce	2 grams	1 dash
golden raisins	300 grams	generous 2 cups
4 to 6 ciabatta rolls (page 83)	--------	--------
1/2 English cucumber, sliced for serving	--------	--------
toasted almond slivers, for serving	60 grams	1/2 cup
thinly sliced purple shiso leaves or micro shiso leaves, for serving	--------	--------

THE SWEET STUFF

Whenever I make any type of pastry, cake, or confectionery, my first question is, "Is it too sweet?"

There is a misconception nowadays that every pastry is full of sugar and that, in fact, that's what makes it a pastry. For me, the skill and artistry that goes into pastry making, like almost anything in life, requires finding the right balance.

I try to treat sugar in pastry like I treat salt in savory food—too much and it's overpowering, too little and the food is bland. It's easy to put caramel or chocolate sauce on top of everything, add marshmallows where they don't belong, douse something in syrup—maybe the first bite is nice, but how do you feel ten minutes later? Sugar produces and gives energy, so our bodies yearn for it. In children, this craving is a survival technique. That's why kids would happily eat a plate of gummy bears, but not necessarily a plate of peas; it's in their DNA. As we get older that natural urge subsides somewhat.

As a pastry chef, I pride myself on a judicious use of sugar. Of course, some things, such as one-bite items like caramels, are sweet by definition, and that's okay because you eat one or two of them at a time—not a whole plateful. But even when creating the recipe for caramels in the confectionary chapter, I posed the question: How do we take something that is 95 percent sugar and make it balanced? I ended up making a beurre noisette out of the butter to create a dark caramel, which gives it a natural bitterness, and then added salt to balance the sweetness. Then I flavor the caramels with ingredients that further balance the sweetness, either with savory items like hazelnuts or something more acidic like passionfruit or mango.

Are the recipes in this chapter sweet? Yes. Are they overly sweet and sickly? No. That's because I've used the natural sweetness that comes from milk, cream, chocolate, and even lemons or honey to avoid employing excessive quantities of refined sugar. My hope is that you will enjoy the results.

PETIT (AND GRAND) GÂTEAUX

Petit gâteux is a fancy way of saying small cakes—traditionally made for individual consumption, which personally I always like so I don't have to share! As with all the recipes in this book, I try to be very conscious about the level of sweetness, but also the amount of flavor they deliver, by which I mean that I want you to be able to taste all of the flavors that are being used in each cake. This is a little more challenging with smaller cakes, but if I serve you a Chocolate Mandarin Mousse, I want you to be able to clearly taste both chocolate and mandarin—not just a hint of citrus that's overwhelmed by the chocolate. If you can't identify the flavors with your eyes closed, for me that's a problem; as with everything it's about finding a balance. Hopefully the recipes that follow achieve that objective. The shapes and sizes described here are guidelines—get creative with what you have around you. The petit Earl Grey and Blood Orange Chocolate Mousse could easily be assembled and served in martini glasses (just put a piece of hazelnut dacquoise in the bottom of each glass, top with the mousse, and chill), or you could make it into one large cake and serve it in slices rather than as individual cakes.

CARROT AND COCONUT CAKE
WITH PISTACHIO AND COCONUT GRANOLA
MAKES ONE 20 X 40-INCH SHEET CAKE OR TWO 8- TO 10-INCH CAKE RINGS, 3 TO 4 INCHES DEEP

This a modern take on a classic cake, the main difference being that I have substituted coconut oil for the more traditional vegetable oil for two reasons. First (and most important) is flavor—this way, you get the flavor of coconut throughout the cake. Second, it's much healthier, so you won't feel as guilty if you eat the whole cake yourself! Swapping out the vegetable oil keeps this cake from becoming greasy or heavy to eat and adds another level of sweetness so we can cut down on the sugar.

The sugared, multicolored baby carrots are not essential, but they do really make a statement if you have the time—plus they're tasty! Note that in this recipe, unlike most traditional carrot cake recipes, there are no spices. This is because I want the carrot and coconut flavors to come through, not be masked by cinnamon and nutmeg or the like.

Preheat the oven to 350°F.

Make the cake: In a stand mixer with a whisk attachment, mix the sugar, coconut oil, and eggs until a smooth paste forms.

In a separate bowl, sift together the flour, baking soda and powder, ginger, and salt. Add the dry ingredients to the wet ingredients and mix to incorporate. Turn off the mixer and fold in the carrots with a spatula until evenly distributed.

Pour the batter into a cake pan or frame lined with parchment paper and bake for 30 to 40 minutes, until a skewer or cake tester comes out clean. Allow the cake to cool completely on a wire rack.

Meanwhile, make the frosting: In a stand mixer fitted with a beater attachment, cream the butter until white and fluffy. Add the cream cheese and vanilla and continue to beat until smooth. Add the confectioners' sugar and beat again until smooth.

Depending on the thickness of your cake, you may want to cut it into two layers and add a layer of cream cheese frosting between them. Spread a layer of frosting over the cake and, before the icing sets, generously cover the icing with the granola and decorate with the dehydrated carrots if you're feeling fancy.

INGREDIENT	WEIGHT	VOLUME
Carrot and Coconut Cake		
sugar	500 grams	2 1/2 cups
unrefined coconut oil	350 grams	1 3/4 cups
5 large eggs	250 grams	1 cup
all-purpose flour	375 grams	3 cups + 2 tablespoons
baking soda	15 grams	3 teaspoons
baking powder	15 grams	3 teaspoons
ground ginger	5 grams	2 1/2 teaspoons
salt	5 grams	3/4 teaspoon
grated carrots	525 grams	4 3/4 cups
Cream Cheese Frosting		
unsalted European-style butter, softened	280 grams	1 1/4 cups
cream cheese, softened	215 grams or 7 1/2 ounces	13 1/2 tablespoons
1 vanilla bean, split in half lengthwise, seeds scraped	--------	--------
confectioners' sugar, sifted	280 grams	2 1/2 cups
For Garnish		
1 recipe coconut and pistachio granola (see opposite page)	--------	--------
candied dehydrated carrots (see opposite page)	--------	--------

COCONUT AND PISTACHIO GRANOLA

MAKES ABOUT 9 CUPS

Make this granola for the carrot cake and then enjoy the leftovers for breakfast. It will last for a few weeks in an airtight container, so feel free to double the recipe so you'll have a backup in the cupboard.

INGREDIENT	WEIGHT	VOLUME
rolled oats	1 kilogram	generous 11 cups
hazelnuts, roughly chopped	150 grams	1 1/3 cups
Sicilian pistachios	100 grams	3/4 cups
unsweetened coconut flakes	100 grams	1 1/4 cups
maple syrup	100 grams	5 tablespoons
honey	100 grams	4 1/2 tablespoons
unrefined coconut oil	100 grams	1/2 cup
golden raisins	100 grams	11 tablespoons
dried cranberries	100 grams	3/4 cup
dried cherries	100 grams	11 tablespoons
chopped dried apricots	100 grams	3/4 cup
ground cinnamon	20 grams	10 teaspoons

Preheat the oven to 350°F.

Place the oats, hazelnuts, pistachios, and coconut flakes in a bowl. Warm the maple syrup, honey, and coconut oil in a saucepan over low heat and pour the syrup over the dry ingredients. Mix to thoroughly coat.

Roast the oat mixture for 10 minutes and stir, followed by another 10 minutes, until a dark roast is achieved.

Allow to cool, then break up the granola into chunks. Add the raisins, cranberries, cherries, apricots, and cinnamon and toss to combine. Store in an airtight bag or container.

CANDIED DEHYDRATED CARROTS

MAKES ABOUT 4 CUPS

INGREDIENT	WEIGHT	VOLUME
10 to 12 organic baby carrots in assorted colors, preferably purple, orange, and yellow	--------	---------
simple syrup (1:1 ratio of sugar to water)	--------	200 ml or 14 tablespoons

Preheat the oven to 180 to 200°F.

Using a new green scouring pad, scrub the peels off the baby carrots (it's much quicker than using a vegetable peeler). Wash the carrots under running water and pat dry.

Using a mandoline with the guard, slice the carrots lengthwise as thinly as possible, then place them directly in the syrup to coat. Arrange the carrot slices in a single layer on a half-sheet pan lined with parchment paper or a silicone mat (see Sources, page 251).

Place the carrots in the oven and then turn it off and leave the carrots in the warm oven overnight, or until the carrots release their liquid and become crisp. Reserve in an airtight container for up to 10 days.

EARL GREY & BLOOD ORANGE CHOCOLATE MOUSSE

WITH HAZELNUT DACQUOISE

SERVES 10 TO 12

Earl Grey tea is made by blending tea leaves with the oil of bergamot, a type of orange grown in Italy and France that gives the tea its pungent smell and taste. To really bring out the bergamot flavor, I add blood orange zest to this recipe. I chose milk chocolate for this mousse so the various flavor notes won't be masked by dark chocolate. Hazelnut dacquoise is a traditional flourless sponge.

Preheat the oven to 380°F.

Make the hazelnut dacquoise: Using a stand mixer with a whisk attachment, whisk the egg whites until they become foamy, then gradually sprinkle in the sugar, whisking on full speed after it's all added until a smooth meringue is achieved.

Using a fine-mesh sieve, sift the hazelnut flour and confectioners' sugar, then using a spatula, fold them into the meringue, mixing gently until fully incorporated.

On a half-sheet pan lined with parchment paper and sprayed with nonstick spray, spread the dacquoise evenly over the pan. Bake for 8 to 12 minutes, until it has a light color and bounces back when you press with your finger. Let cool on a wire rack.

Meanwhile, make the mousse: Soak the gelatin sheets in cold water until soft; drain and squeeze out excess water.

Put the tea in a small saucepan and add water just to cover. Bring to a boil and continue to boil until the water has evaporated.

TIP: Cooking the tea leaves slightly helps rehydrate them and removes some of the strong tannin flavors, like you would get from overbrewing tea.

As soon as the pan is dry, add the milk, bring to just under a boil, then strain over the egg yolks and sugar, whisking continuously.

Return to a clean pan and stir with a spatula in a figure eight motion until the crème anglaise begins to thicken; remove immediately from the heat, add the drained gelatin, and pass through a fine-mesh sieve, directly over the chocolate. Stir until the chocolate is fully melted.

In three stages, gently fold in the whipped cream until fully incorporated. Add the zest of the blood oranges.

Line a 9-inch cake ring (2 inches deep) or 10-inch frame (2 inches deep) by gently pressing the ring or frame over the cooked dacquoise and cutting around the ring or frame so you have a tight-fitting base, exactly the same size. Lightly spray the sides of the ring or the frame with nonstick spray so it is easier to unmold after it has set.

Pour the mousse into the mold or cake ring over the hazelnut dacquoise, place in the refrigerator, and allow a minimum of 4 to 5 hours to set, but ideally overnight.

To finish the mousse, remove it from the mold or cake ring, ensuring that the dacquoise is on its base, and place in the freezer for at least 3 or 4 hours, but preferably overnight.

Meanwhile, make the chocolate glaze: In a saucepan, combine the cream, milk, and neutral glaze and bring to a boil. Pour the hot cream mixture over the chocolate and mix well, emulsifying with a whisk or hand blender. Transfer to a heatproof container and allow the glaze to set up in the refrigerator.

When you're ready to assemble the mousse, gently melt the chocolate glaze in the microwave; it's ready to use when it reaches 95°F. (If you don't have a thermometer, then wait until the glaze is around body temperature before using.)

Remove the mousse from the freezer and place it on a cooling rack set over a half-sheet pan or parchment paper to catch the drips. Pour the glaze over the mousse, allowing the excess to run off, then immediately place the mousse on a plate and return it to the refrigerator to allow the glaze to set.

When ready to serve, add one or two blood orange macarons (page 161) and some caramelized hazelnuts (page 69), if you like.

INGREDIENT	WEIGHT	VOLUME
Hazelnut Dacquoise		
9 large egg whites	450 grams	1 3/4 cups
granulated sugar	120 grams	9 1/2 tablespoons
hazelnut flour or ground hazelnuts	375 grams	4 1/4 cups
confectioners' sugar	375 grams	3 1/4 cups
Mousse		
6 sheets gelatin	12 grams	--------
loose Earl Grey tea	40 grams	10 tablespoons
milk	375 grams	generous 1 1/2 cups
5 large egg yolks	90 grams	generous 1/3 cup
granulated sugar	60 grams	5 tablespoons
milk chocolate, preferably Valrhona Jivara Lactee pistoles or bars *(see Sources, page 250)*	450 grams or 16 ounces	2 2/3 cups chopped, if using chocolate bars
heavy cream, whipped to soft peaks	450 grams	scant 2 cups
zest of 3 blood oranges	--------	--------
Chocolate Glaze		
heavy cream	300 grams	generous 1 1/4 cups
milk	375 grams	generous 1 1/2 cups
neutral glaze *(see Sources, page 250)*	50 grams	2 2/3 tablespoons
dark semisweet chocolate, preferably Valrhona Manjari pistoles or bars *(64% cacao; see Sources, page 250)*	500 grams or 17 1/2 ounces	scant 3 cups chopped, if using chocolate bars

SUMMER FRUIT TARTS

MAKES TEN 3- OR 3 1/2-INCH TARTLETS

This recipe calls for summer fruits, such as apricots, strawberries, blueberries, and/or raspberries, but most soft fruits will work nicely atop these tarts. Feel free to change the size and quantity of tarts as well.

Soak the gelatin in cold water until soft; drain and squeeze out excess water.

In a large metal bowl, combine the eggs, lemon and yuzu juices, and sugar. Create a double boiler by bringing a few inches of water to a simmer in a pan and then placing the metal bowl over the water, making sure the bowl doesn't actually touch the water. Immediately start to whisk without stopping (otherwise you will have scrambled eggs) until the egg and sugar mixture has thickened and begins to hold its shape. Remove from the heat and whisk in the drained gelatin.

Allow to cool for 5 minutes and then whisk in the cubed butter until the mixture is emulsified. Transfer to a plastic bowl or storage container, and cover with plastic wrap, making sure it is touching the surface of the curd, then reserve in the refrigerator until cool.

To assemble the tartlets, remove the sweet pastry from the refrigerator and allow it to temper at room temperature for at least 1 hour. (Do not place it in direct sunlight or anywhere else that might be too hot.)

Line a large baking sheet with parchment paper and place ten 3- to 3 1/2-inch metal ring molds on top, spacing them out evenly.

Lightly flour a work surface and, using a rolling pin, roll out the pastry until it's approximately 1/8 inch thick.

Working quickly and carefully, roll the dough around the rolling pin, so you can lift it without it breaking, and then unroll it over the prepared tart rings.

Using a small sharp knife, cut around each ring mold, leaving at least a 3/4-inch margin of dough around each ring.

INGREDIENT	WEIGHT	VOLUME
1 recipe sweet pastry (page 185)	--------	--------
Lemon and Yuzu Curd		
3 sheets of gelatin	6 grams	--------
10 large eggs	500 grams	2 cups
freshly squeezed lemon juice	200 grams	13 tablespoons
yuzu juice	40 grams	2 1/2 tablespoons
sugar	550 grams	2 3/4 cups
cold unsalted European-style butter, cut into cubes	750 grams	3 1/3 cups
assortment of summer fruits, such as blueberries, raspberries, hulled and sliced strawberries, pitted and sliced apricots	about 500 grams	about 2 cups

Using your thumb and forefinger, gently push the dough into the sides of a ring mold, working clockwise. Repeat for each mold. Using gentle pressure, roll the rolling pin over all the rings, cutting off all the excess dough and leaving you with ten perfectly lined ring molds. Reserve the trimmings for another day, and place the lined ring molds in the fridge to rest for 1 hour.

Preheat a convection oven to 350°F or a standard oven to 325°F.

Remove the ring molds from the refrigerator and line each one with a square of parchment paper, roughly double its diameter, so the edges hang over the sides. Fill the molds to the top with baking beans (raw rice or dried beans also work perfectly well for this), press down, and then seal in the beans with the excess parchment paper, so they look like small parcels inside the ring mold.

If using a convection oven, turn the fan to low and bake for 10 to 12 minutes, until the pastry is cooked and has a light, golden color. If using a standard oven, bake for 8 to 10 minutes and check if the pastry is cooked; rotate and adjust the baking time as necessary.

Allow the pastry to cool in the molds. Once cool, remove the baking beans and parchment paper, and gently lift the cooked pastry shell from each ring mold.

Using a small spatula, fill each tart shell with the chilled lemon-yuzu curd and flatten off the tops with the edge of a palette knife so the tops of the tarts are completely smooth.

Top each tartlet off with the summer fruits of your choice and enjoy!

CHOCOLATE MANDARIN MOUSSE

SERVES 8

If you bring out this dessert at a dinner party, even your fussiest friend will be impressed. It looks much harder to make than it is. It does require a special half-sphere-shaped mold, but they're available online and the multipurpose shape means you can use it for many other recipes in this book. If you want to get really fancy, serve this mousse with a few mandarins with stems attached, and see who spots it first.

INGREDIENT	WEIGHT	VOLUME
Mandarin Mousse		
3 sheets gelatin	6 grams	--------
milk	190 grams	12 1/2 tablespoons
zest of 3 mandarins	--------	--------
2 large egg yolks	40 grams	2 1/2 tablespoons
sugar	30 grams	2 1/2 tablespoons
milk chocolate, preferably Valrhona Bahibé pistoles or bars (46% cacao; see Sources, page 250)	225 grams or 8 ounces	1 1/3 cups chopped, if using chocolate bars
mandarin juice	25 grams	1 2/3 tablespoons
heavy cream, whipped to soft peaks	225 grams	scant 1 cup

Soak the gelatin sheets in cold water; drain and then squeeze out excess water.

In a saucepan, bring the milk and mandarin zest just to a boil. In a large bowl, whisk together the egg yolks and sugar. Whisking continuously, pour the boiling milk over the eggs and sugar.

Return to a clean pan and stir with a spatula in a figure eight motion until the crème anglaise begins to thicken; remove immediately from the heat, add the drained gelatin, and pass it through a fine-mesh sieve, directly over the chocolate. Stir until the chocolate is fully melted, then stir in the mandarin juice. Allow to cool.

In three stages, gently fold in the whipped cream until fully incorporated.

Using a piping bag or spoon, fill sixteen 3-inch half-sphere molds three-quarters full. Place in the freezer for at least 3 to 4 hours, or until frozen.

When frozen solid, push a mousse out of its mold and place the two flat sides together. Working quickly and using your fingers to smooth, join the two edges together so you have a perfectly smooth sphere. Return to the freezer. Repeat with the remaining frozen mousse. Insert large wooden skewers into the middle of each sphere of mousse; leave them in the freezer.

INGREDIENT	WEIGHT	VOLUME
Mandarin Glaze		
9 sheets gelatin	18 grams	--------
mandarin purée (see Sources, page 251)	250 grams	1 cup + 6 1/2 tablespoons
glucose or corn syrup (see Sources, page 251)	40 grams	2 tablespoons
orange liquid food coloring	2 grams	scant 1/2 teaspoon

Soak the gelatin in cold water until soft; drain and squeeze out excess water.

Heat the mandarin purée and glucose in a saucepan. When hot, add the drained gelatin, whisk to incorporate, and then pass through a fine-mesh sieve. Reserve at 95°F (or body temperature, if you don't have a thermometer) until needed.

To assemble the dessert, pour the warm glaze into a deep pitcher. (First make sure the temperature is around 95°F and that the glaze is not too thick; if it is, place it briefly in the microwave until it is liquid again.)

Using the skewer as a handle, quickly dip one of the frozen mousse spheres into the glaze, coating it completely, then quickly remove it to allow the excess glaze to drip off. Immediately dip the sphere again—the glaze should set straightaway. Carefully pull out the skewer and reserve the sphere in the refrigerator until serving time. Repeat with the remaining frozen mousse spheres.

If available, insert some fresh mandarin orange stems with leaves into the holes made by the skewers. Serve on dessert plates at room temperature.

STRAWBERRY CHEESECAKE

SERVES 10

I love this recipe for crust-free, no-bake cheesecake because it's light—not heavy to eat like a traditional cheesecake. Any fruit can be used, but it doesn't get much better than local in-season strawberries.

INGREDIENT	WEIGHT	VOLUME
sliced organic local strawberries, to garnish	--------	--------
Cheesecake		
8 sheets gelatin	16 grams	--------
cream cheese	500 grams	scant 2 cups
sugar	120 grams	9 1/2 tablespoons
10 egg yolks	180 grams	scant 3/4 cup
Frangelico hazelnut liqueur	150 grams	10 tablespoons
heavy cream	500 grams	2 cups + 2 tablespoons

Soak the gelatin sheets in cold water until soft.

In a stand mixer with a beater attachment, paddle the cream cheese until there are no lumps. Add the sugar and continue paddling until the mixture is light and fluffy.

In a separate bowl, whisk the yolks until they reach the ribbon stage. Add the yolks to the cream cheese and mix to combine.

In a small saucepan, warm the Frangelico. Drain the gelatin, squeeze out excess water, and melt the gelatin in the Frangelico.

With the mixer on medium speed, stream the Frangelico into the cream cheese mixture and then gradually mix in the heavy cream. Strain the cheesecake filling through a fine-mesh sieve and then pour it into an 8-inch pie pan or other mold of your choice (photo shows a small individual cheesecake made with a 3-inch mold on a sablé Breton cookie). Place in the freezer for at least 3 hours or overnight. Meanwhile, make the strawberry glaze.

INGREDIENT	WEIGHT	VOLUME
Strawberry Glaze		
6 sheets gelatin	12 grams	--------
strawberry purée	250 grams	1 cup + 1 tablespoon
glucose or corn syrup (see Sources, page 251)	25 grams	3 1/2 teaspoons
sugar	160 grams	generous 3/4 cup
pectin (see Sources, page 251)	4 grams	1 1/4 teaspoons
citric acid (see Sources, page 250)	3 grams	1/2 teaspoon

Soak the gelatin in cold water until soft; drain and squeeze out excess water.

In a small saucepan, bring the strawberry purée, glucose, and 60 grams (generous 1/4 cup) of the sugar to a boil.

In a bowl, whisk together the pectin and the remaining 100 grams (1/2 cup) of sugar. Whisk the pectin and sugar mixture into the strawberry purée mixture so there are no lumps. Continue to whisk for 1 minute more and then whisk in the citric acid and drained gelatin.

Let cool slightly before using the glaze.

When you're ready to assemble the dessert: Place the glaze in a metal bowl and melt over a pan of simmering water. When the glaze has melted, pour it over the frozen cheesecake, transfer to a plate, and allow 10 to 15 minutes for the cheesecake to come to room temperature before slicing and serving.

SABLÉ BRETON

MAKES 20 COOKIES

INGREDIENT	WEIGHT	VOLUME
sugar	120 grams	1/2 cup + 5 teaspoons
salted European-style butter	200 grams	1/2 cup + 6 tablespoons
3 egg yolks	60 grams	1/4 cup
vanilla extract	--------	1 tablespoon
all-purpose flour, preferably King Arthur Sir Galahad artisan flour	280 grams	2 cups + 5 tablespoons *(plus additional for rolling)*

Preheat the oven to 375°F.

In a stand mixer with a paddle attachment, beat the butter and sugar together until light in color and fluffy, about 3 minutes.

Add two of the egg yolks and the vanilla extract and beat on a medium speed until incorporated. Stop the mixer and scrape down the sides of the bowl to the center, using a rubber spatula. Add the flour and mix on a low speed until the dough just comes together.

Lightly flour your work surface and place the dough on top, bring it together into a ball using your hands, sprinkle the top with some additional flour, and using a rolling pin, roll out until it's around 1/3 inch thick.

Using a 3 1/2- to 4-inch cookie cutter, cut out circles and place on a lined half-sheet pan, roughly 12 to a tray; prick each cookie with a fork.

Whisk up the remaining egg yolk and brush the top of the cookies. Bake for 12 to 15 minutes, until a golden brown color, then transfer tray to a cooling rack to cool completely.

Place a small individual cheesecake on top of a cookie and finish with sliced strawberries.

CHOUX PASTRY

Choux pastry, or pâte à choux, is a simple recipe, made with four ingredients—butter, flour, water, and eggs. No raising agent, such as yeast, is added; instead it relies on the steam created from the eggs and water during the baking process to make the pastry rise. The name *choux* comes from the French word for cabbage; apparently back in the 1500s when these pastries were first made they looked like mini cabbages, and so pâte à choux was born.

What I love about making pâte à choux is its versatility. In this chapter I show you how to make éclairs, choux buns, and chouquettes. From there, the flavor combinations are endless.

CHOUX PASTRY

MAKES 35 TO 40 ÉCLAIRS OR 60 TO 70 CHOUQUETTES

This is a large recipe—make it and bake it or freeze it until you need it.

In a large pan, combine the water, butter, sugar, and salt and bring to a boil. Add the flour and mix well using a stiff spatula, then cook on a moderate heat for about 10 minutes, until a dry ball forms.

TIP: This process will release a lot of steam. It's important that the resulting ball of paste is dry; if it's too wet, it will not be able to accept all the eggs and your dough will be too wet to rise.

Place the dry ball in a stand mixer with a beater attachment and mix on a medium speed for 1 to 2 minutes, until the first lot of steam is gone. Gradually beat in the eggs, stopping the mixer frequently to check the consistency of the dough as you go before adding them all.

TIP: You may not need to add all the eggs. When you stop the mixer to check the consistency, scoop up some of the mixture on your spatula and let it fall back into the bowl—if it's a constant stream, continue to add more of the eggs. If it's thick enough to hold its own shape and breaks up when you drop it from the spatula, you are done.

When cool, transfer the pastry dough to a plastic bowl, cover with plastic wrap, and allow to rest in the refrigerator overnight.

TIP: This step is not imperative, but chilling the dough overnight creates a better consistency and temperature for piping.

INGREDIENT	WEIGHT	VOLUME
water	750 grams	750 milliliters or 3 cups + 3 tablespoons
unsalted European-style butter	375 grams	1 2/3 cups
superfine sugar	30 grams	2 1/2 tablespoons
fine sea salt	8 grams	1 3/4 teaspoons
all-purpose flour, ideally King Arthur Sir Galahad artisan flour, sifted through a fine-mesh sieve	500 grams	4 cups + 3 tablespoons
14 large eggs	700 grams	2 3/4 cups
egg wash (1 egg/50 grams to 2 tablespoons water)	--------	--------

PIPE THE
CHOUX PASTRY

Line half-sheet pans with parchment paper, then pipe the desired shape as described below.

For éclairs: Fill a fluted-tip piping bag with the choux pastry. In one motion, pipe 6-inch long strips on the parchment paper. Usng your finger and some water, gently tidy up the ends of the éclairs so they are round and smooth.

TIP: To help with accuracy, using a pencil, mark a few sheets of parchment paper with rows of 6-inch straight lines. You can use these as your guidelines as you pipe.

When one half-sheet pan is full, spray the tops of the éclairs with nonstick cooking spray. Repeat with the remaining pans and choux.

For chouquettes: Fill a straight-tip piping bag with the dough. Holding the bag vertically, pipe small circles, each a little larger than a quarter coin or roughly 1 inch.

When one half-sheet pan is complete, brush the tops with egg wash and sprinkle with pearl sugar (see Sources, page 251). Repeat with the remaining pans and choux.

BAKE THE
CHOUX PASTRY

Place a small tray of water in the bottom of the oven. (This will create additional steam to help the pastry rise.) Preheat the oven to 375°F.

TIP: Steam is vital to the success of any item made with choux pastry. When the pastry goes into the oven, it is important that the oven door remains closed until the second round of baking is complete, as described below.

Bake for 20 minutes, then reduce the oven temperature to 325°F (but do not open the door) and bake for another 20 minutes. For the third round of baking, reduce the oven temperature to 300°F, open the door slightly to release any excess steam, then close the door and bake for another 20 minutes, or until the pastry is crisp and golden.

Allow to cool on a wire rack.

CHOUX
PASTRY

1 Begin to boil the water, butter, sugar, and salt

2 Add all the flour at once

3 Using a wooden spoon, begin to beat the flour into the liquid

4 Continue to beat over a medium heat

5 Beat until the dough has formed a ball, and has dried out slightly

6 Place hot dough in a stand mixer with the beater attachment

7 When the dough has cooled slightly, gradually add the eggs, one by one

8 Beat on medium speed until cool

CHOUX
PASTRY

9 Place in a plastic piping bag

10 With a straight tip, pipe chouquettes

11 With a fluted tip, pipe éclairs

DARK CHOCOLATE ÉCLAIRS

MAKES 10 TO 12 ÉCLAIRS

When people ask me what my favorite pastry is to eat, éclairs are always near the top of my list. It may just be nostalgia, taking me back to when I was a child gazing longingly into the pâtisserie cases in France. Out of all of the petit gâteaux, I would always choose an éclair. This version, filled with dark chocolate mousse, is one of the classics.

INGREDIENT	WEIGHT	VOLUME
10 to 12 baked and cooled éclairs (see Choux Pastry recipe, page 134)	--------	--------
Dark Chocolate Mousse		
3 sheets gelatin	6 grams	--------
milk	190 grams	generous 3/4 cup
2 large egg yolks	40 grams	2 1/2 tablespoons
sugar	30 grams	2 1/2 tablespoons
dark semisweet chocolate, ideally Valrhona Manjari pistoles or bars (64% cacao; see Sources, page 250)	225 grams or 8 ounces	1 1/3 cups chopped, if using chocolate bars
heavy cream, whipped to soft peaks	225 grams	scant 1 cup

Soak the gelatin sheets in cold water until soft; drain and squeeze out excess water.

In a saucepan, bring the milk to a boil. In a large bowl, whisk together the egg yolks and sugar. Whisking continually, pour the milk over the eggs and sugar.

Return to a clean pan and stir with a spatula in a figure eight motion until the crème anglaise begins to thicken; remove immediately from the heat, add the drained gelatin, and pass through a fine-mesh sieve, directly over the chocolate. Stir until the chocolate is fully melted.

When cool, in three stages, gently fold in the whipped cream until incorporated. Pour into piping bags and allow to set in the refrigerator for a minimum of 4 to 5 hours and up to 3 days.

INGREDIENT	WEIGHT	VOLUME
Chocolate Glaze		
10 sheets gelatin	20 grams	--------
cocoa powder, such as Valrhona brand	50 grams	7 tablespoons
water	175 grams	3/4 cup
heavy cream	170 grams	scant 3/4 cup
sugar	320 grams	1 1/2 cups + 2 tablespoons

Soak the gelatin sheets in cold water until soft; drain and squeeze out excess water.

In a saucepan, combine the cocoa powder, water, cream, and sugar and bring to a boil, whisking to combine. Add the drained gelatin, whisking until thickened. Remove from the heat and set aside until you're ready to glaze.

To assemble the éclairs, using a small round pastry tip, punch three evenly spaced holes into the base of the baked éclairs.

TIP: This is done so that when it comes to filling the éclairs you can get an evenly distributed filling throughout the éclair—if you just filled from one end, for example, you risk breaking the éclair and not filling it all the way through.

Attach the same small round tip to a piping bag with the chocolate mousse.

Pipe the mousse into the cavities of an éclair until completely full. Repeat with the remaining éclairs.

TIP: When the éclair is full, you should be able to feel its heft. If it feels light, add some more filling.

To glaze the éclairs, reheat the chocolate glaze to 90°F.

Holding the base of an éclair, dip the top into the glaze until it reaches the middle of the éclair. Using your finger, swipe any excess glaze off the top and allow it to drip off the éclair. Repeat with the remaining éclairs and glaze.

Place the éclairs in the refrigerator to allow the glaze to set. These are best consumed on the same day they're filled.

PARIS-BREST ÉCLAIRS

MAKES 15 ÉCLAIRS

The classic Paris-Brest is traditionally a large ring made of choux pastry filled with coffee pastry cream, flaked almonds, and whipped cream. It was created in honor of a much-loved bicycle race that went from Paris to the town of Brest at the most western tip of France, then back again. The round ring shape signifies the wheel of a bike. To make this pastry more manageable to eat, here it is transformed into an éclair.

In a saucepan, heat the milk and cream to just under a boil. In a bowl, mix together the sugar and cornstarch. Add the egg yolks and whisk until well combined.

Add a little of the hot milk to the egg mixture, then slowly pour all of the mixture into the hot milk in the pan. Bring to a boil and whisk moderately until the custard begins to thicken. Reduce the heat and cook for another minute, whisking vigorously.

Put the custard into the bowl of a stand mixer and paddle for about 5 minutes to cool slightly. Add the butter and espresso and mix for another 5 minutes, until the pastry cream is smooth and glossy. Pour into a plastic container and cover with plastic wrap so it's touching the surface.

To assemble the éclairs, using a small round pastry tip, punch three evenly spaced holes into the base of the baked éclairs. (See the first tip on the opposite page.)

Attach the same small round tip to a piping bag and fill it with the coffee pastry cream. Pipe the cream into the cavities of an éclair until completely full. (See the second tip on the opposite page.) Repeat with the remaining éclairs.

To glaze the éclairs, reheat the chocolate glaze to 90°F.

Holding the base of an éclair, dip the top into the glaze until it reaches the middle of the éclair. Using your finger, swipe any excess glaze off the top and allow it to drip off the éclair. Repeat with the remaining éclairs and glaze. Place the éclairs in the refrigerator to allow the glaze to set.

To finish, put some of the coffee pastry cream in another piping bag with a small round pastry tip. Working widthwise from left to right, pipe a tight zigzag across the top of an éclair. Repeat with the remaining éclairs. Sprinkle liberally with toasted flaked almonds and dust with confectioners' sugar.

INGREDIENT	WEIGHT	VOLUME
15 baked and cooled éclairs	--------	--------
(see Choux Pastry recipe, page 134)		
Coffee Pastry Cream		
milk	320 grams	1 1/3 cups
heavy cream	320 grams	1 cup + 6 tablespoons
sugar	160 grams	generous 3/4 cup
cornstarch	45 grams	1/3 cup
7 large egg yolks	128 grams	1/2 cup
cold unsalted European-style butter, cut into cubes	80 grams	5 tablespoons + 2 teaspoons
2 shots espresso	--------	--------
For Garnish		
1 recipe Chocolate Glaze	--------	--------
(see opposite page)		
toasted flaked almonds	--------	--------
confectioners' sugar, for dusting	--------	--------

THE SWEET STUFF

SICILIAN PISTACHIO ÉCLAIRS

MAKES 12 TO 15 ÉCLAIRS

Why feature Sicilian pistachios? They are expensive—only small amounts of them are produced on the island of Sicily—but their flavor and color set them apart. Grown in volcanic soil, Sicilian pistachios are a vibrant green and have a much sharper taste than their Middle Eastern counterparts.

INGREDIENT	WEIGHT	VOLUME
12 to 15 baked and cooled éclairs (see Choux Pastry recipe, page 134)	--------	--------
Sicilian Pistacho Pastry Cream		
milk	320 grams	1 1/3 cups
heavy cream	320 grams	1 cup + 6 tablespoons
salt	3 grams	1/2 teaspoon
natural pistachio paste (see Sources, page 251)	40 grams	8 teaspoons
sweetened pistachio paste (see Sources, page 251)	50 grams	10 teaspoons
sugar	160 grams	generous 3/4 cup
cornstarch	45 grams	1/3 cup
7 large egg yolks	130 grams	1/2 cup
cold unsalted European-style butter, cut into cubes	80 grams	5 tablespoons + 2 teaspoons

In a saucepan, heat the milk and cream with the salt and both pistachio pastes.

In a bowl, mix together the sugar and cornstarch. Add the egg yolks and whisk until combined.

Add a little of the hot milk to the egg mixture, then slowly pour all of the egg mixture into the hot milk in the pan. Bring to a boil and whisk moderately until the custard begins to thicken. Reduce the heat and cook for another minute, whisking vigorously.

Put the custard into the bowl of a stand mixer and paddle for about 5 minutes to cool slightly. Add the butter and mix for another 5 minutes, until smooth and glossy. Pour into a plastic container and cover with plastic wrap so it's touching the surface.

Let cool in the refrigerator until needed.

INGREDIENT	WEIGHT	VOLUME
Pistachio Ganache Glaze		
white chocolate, preferably Valrhona Opalys pistoles or bars (33% cacao; see Sources, page 250)	200 grams or 7 ounces	1 cup + 3 tablespoons chopped, if using chocolate bars
heavy cream	150 grams	2/3 cup
sweetened and green-colored pistachio paste (see Sources, page 251)	30 grams	2 tablespoons
glucose or corn syrup (see Sources, page 251)	20 grams	2 3/4 teaspoons
neutral glaze (see Sources, page 250)	200 grams	2/3 cup

Melt the white chocolate in a metal bowl over a pan of simmering water. Be careful not to allow the white chocolate to burn.

In a medium saucepan over a medium heat, boil the cream, pistachio paste, glucose syrup, and neutral glaze.

Pour the hot cream mixture over the chocolate, whisking until emulsified, ideally using a hand blender. Be sure to minimize air bubbles. Use straightaway or cover with plastic wrap and store in the refrigerator.

To assemble the éclairs, using a small round pastry tip, punch three evenly spaced holes into the base of the baked éclairs.

TIP: We do this so that when it comes to filling the eclairs you can get an evenly distributed filling throughout the éclair—if you just filled from one end, for example, you risk breaking the éclair and not filling it all the way through.

Attach the same small round tip to a piping bag and fill it with the pastry cream. Pipe the cream into the cavities of an éclair until completely full. Repeat with the remaining éclairs.

TIP: When the éclair is full, you should be able to feel its heft. If it feels light, add some more filling.

To glaze the éclairs, reheat the white chocolate glaze to 90°F.

Holding the base of an éclair, dip the top into the glaze until it reaches the middle of the éclair. Using your finger, swipe any excess glaze off the top and allow it to drip off. Repeat with the remaining éclairs and glaze.

Place the éclairs in the refrigerator to allow the glaze to set. These are best consumed on the same day they're filled.

CRAQUELIN-TOPPED CREAM PUFFS

MAKES 40 TO 50 CREAM PUFFS

These sweet and crunchy cream puffs are addictive and welcomed at pretty much any occasion. Utilize any leftover pâte à choux or just make a whole recipe and snack on them all day! The craquelin on top not only helps create a perfect round shape and prevents cracking, but also gives them a sweet crunchy texture.

Make the craquelin: Combine all the ingredients in a stand mixer with the paddle attachment, and mix on a medium speed until the mix has come together to form a smooth ball.

Using a rolling pin, roll out the dough between two sheets of parchment paper until paper thin. Reserve in the freezer.

When you're ready to bake, preheat a convection or regular oven to 350°F. Transfer the dough and parchment to a work surface and remove the top sheet of parchment. Using a small ring cutter, about 1 inch in diameter, punch out 40 to 50 discs.

Place one disk on top of each piped chouquette and bake in the oven on a half-sheet pan on a low fan speed for 10 to 12 minutes, until the cream puffs are fully risen and the tops are a deep golden color. Remove from the oven and allow to cool directly on the half-sheet pan—once completely cool, use straightaway or transfer to zip-tight plastic bags and freeze for up to three months.

INGREDIENT	WEIGHT	VOLUME
1 recipe chouquettes *(see Choux Pastry recipe, page 134)*, through piping	--------	--------
Craquelin		
cold unsalted Europen-style butter, cubed	300 grams	1 1/3 cups
demerara *(natural cane sugar)*	300 grams	1 cup + 7 tablespoons
all-purpose flour, preferably King Arthur Sir Galahad artisan flour	300 grams	2 1/2 cups

RASPBERRY & ROSE ÉCLAIRS

MAKES 12 TO 15 ÉCLAIRS

This recipe is inspired by éclairs I've enjoyed in Paris, specifically Pierre Hermé's creations; this is a version of one of his classic flavor pairings that is simply delicious.

INGREDIENT	WEIGHT	VOLUME
12 to 15 baked and cooled éclairs (see Choux Pastry recipe, page 134)	--------	--------
Rose Crème Chiboust		
6 sheets gelatin	12 grams	--------
heavy cream	200 grams	14 tablespoons
milk	100 grams	6 2/3 tablespoons
milk powder	35 grams	4 1/2 tablespoons
6 1/2 large egg yolks	120 grams	7 1/2 tablespoons
granulated sugar	100 grams	1/2 cup
water	50 grams	3 tablespoons + 1 teaspoon
cornstarch	50 grams	6 tablespoons
5 large egg whites	160 grams	2/3 cup
superfine sugar	210 grams	1 cup + 1 tablespoon
Monin rose syrup (see Sources, page 250)	50 grams	10 teaspoons
freeze-dried raspberries (see Sources page 250)	30 grams	1/4 cup

INGREDIENT	WEIGHT	VOLUME
Raspberry Ganache Glaze		
white chocolate, preferably Valrhona Opalys pistoles or bars (33% cacao; see Sources, page 250)	200 grams or 7 ounces	1 cup + 3 tablespoons chopped, if using chocolate bars
heavy cream	150 grams	2/3 cup
raspberry purée	30 grams	2 tablespoons
glucose or corn syrup (see Sources, page 251)	20 grams	2 3/4 teaspoons
neutral glaze (see Sources, page 250)	200 grams	2/3 cup
For Garnish		
fresh rose petals	--------	--------
Valrhona white chocolate crispies (see Sources, page 250)	--------	--------

Soak the gelatin in cold water until soft; drain and squeeze out excess water.

Cook a pastry cream by bringing the cream, milk, milk powder, granulated sugar, and cornstarch to a boil, stirring constantly—the mix will thicken as the cornstarch cooks, this must boil for at least 2 minutes, in order to cook out the raw flour taste. (If you don't do this you will have a floury tasting pastry cream.) When the mixture has thickened and boiled for 2 minutes, transfer to the bowl of a stand mixer with a whisk attachment, begin whisking on a low speed and add the egg yolks, followed by the soaked gelatin.

Cook the superfine sugar and water at 250°F and pour slowly over the egg whites to make an Italian meringue. Add the rose syrup and whisk until thickened, but do not let cool down.

While still warm, fold into the pastry cream, whisk to combine, and allow to cool. When cool, scoop into a plastic pastry bag.

Melt the white chocolate in a metal bowl over a pan of simmering water. Be careful not to allow the white chocolate to burn.

In a medium saucepan over a medium heat, boil the cream, raspberry purée, glucose syrup, and neutral glaze.

Pour the hot cream mixture over the chocolate, whisking until emulsified, ideally using a hand blender. Be sure to minimize air bubbles. Use straightaway or cover with plastic wrap and store in the refrigerator.

To assemble the éclairs, using a small round pastry tip, punch three evenly spaced holes into the base of the baked éclairs.

TIP: We do this so that when it comes to filling the éclairs you can get an evenly distributed filling throughout the éclair—if you just filled from one end, for example, you risk breaking the éclair and not filling it all the way through.

Attach the same small round tip to the piping bag with the rose crème chiboust. Pipe the chiboust into the cavities of an éclair until completely full. Repeat with the remaining éclairs.

TIP: When the éclair is full, you should be able to feel its heft. If it feels light, add some more filling.

To glaze the éclairs, reheat the white chocolate glaze to 90°F.

Holding the base of an éclair, dip the top into the glaze until it reaches the middle of the éclair. Using your finger, swipe any excess glaze off the top and allow it to drip off, sprinkle with the freeze-dried raspberries to garnish.

Repeat with the remaining éclairs and glaze.

Place the éclairs in the refrigerator to allow the glaze to set for at least 1 hour. These are best consumed on the same day they're filled. To finish, add the rose petals and chocolate crispies.

THE COMPLEX WORLD OF THE MACARON

Not difficult to make in theory, macarons can be temperamental, but once you've mastered them, they are deeply satisfying. Two meringue shells are sandwiched together with a flavorful filling; the shell should be crisp and fragile, while the middle should be chewy.

Although the possibilities are endless, I've shared some of my favorite flavor combinations in this chapter, but feel free to experiment once you have a handle on the basics. I like ganaches and jams or caramels for the fillings. Personally, I try to avoid using buttercream here, as I find it too rich, but you might enjoy it. Whatever filling you choose, just be aware of how sweet it is, because the shell is 50 percent sugar.

To a large extent, your oven will dictate the success of these little treats. The first time you make them, I suggest that you bake one sheet at a time. That way, you can see how the first macarons come out and make adjustments accordingly. Opening the oven door or moving the pan during baking can have a negative effect; just keep them on the middle rack to allow the most even cooking.

Some good news: Macarons are actually better after they have been frozen. Even if you don't choose to freeze them, they require a few hours in the refrigerator before serving. The moisture of the fridge softens the shell, so the shell cracks but does not shatter; the moisture also make the center chewy, not crunchy.

With a little patience and care, you can make all kinds of beautiful macarons at home.

MACARON
SHELLS

1 Place the sugar in a small saucepan

2 Add powdered color or gel

3 Add enough water to create a texture similar to wet sand and cook the sugar to 250°F

4 Meanwhile, mix half of the egg whites with the almonds and confectioners' sugar

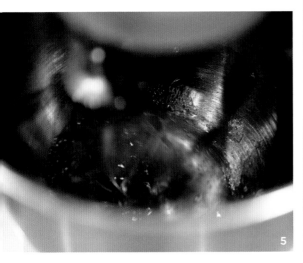

5 In a stand mixer, slowly begin to whisk the remaining egg whites

6 Mix the egg whites with the almond mixture

7 Mix until a paste has been formed, then cover with plastic wrap

MACARON
SHELLS

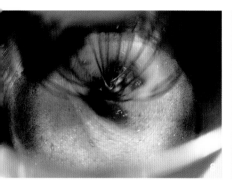

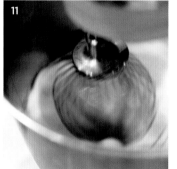

8 Increase the speed of the mixer

9 Gradually sprinkle in the small amount of sugar

10 Heat the sugar syrup to 250°F

11 Reduce the speed of the mixer

12 Gradually add the sugar syrup while the mixer is moving, being careful not to let the syrup touch the whisk

13 Increase the speed and whisk until the batter has doubled in volume and cooled slightly

14 Begin to beat (by hand) the cooked meringue into the almond paste

15 Carefully place the batter in a piping bag fitted with a pastry tip

16 Pipe macaron circles, avoiding any tips on top of the macaron

THE SWEET STUFF

CASSIS & ELDERFLOWER MACARONS
MAKES AT LEAST 25 MACARONS

Cassis is the French term for black currants. These small berries are super sour and grow wild, along with elderflowers, in the woods across Europe. The floral notes of the elderflower and the sharpness of the cassis complement each other perfectly, making this my favorite macaron flavor pairing.

INGREDIENT	WEIGHT	VOLUME
1 recipe Macaron Shells *(page 152)*	--------	--------
purple liquid food coloring or gel *(see Sources, page 250)*	3 grams	1/2 teaspoon
Cassis and Elderflower Crémeux		
cassis or black currant purée *(see Sources, page 250)*	400 grams	1 3/4 cups
water	20 grams	4 teaspoons
3 sheets gelatin	6 grams	--------
3 1/2 large egg yolks	60 grams	3 tablespoons + 2 teaspoons
sugar	50 grams	1/4 cup
cornstarch	25 grams	3 tablespoons
European-style unsalted butter, cut into cubes	250 grams	1 cup + 2 tablespoons
elderflower cordial	50 grams	3 1/2 tablespoons

Prepare the macaron shells using the purple food coloring. Bake and let cool.

Make the crémeux: In a saucepan, heat the cassis until just boiling. Soak the gelatin in cold water until soft; drain and squeeze out excess water.

In a large bowl, whisk together the egg yolks, sugar, and cornstarch. Pour the boiling cassis over the egg mixture and return to the heat in a clean pan, whisking continuously until the mixture has just come to a boil and has thickened. Immediately pour into a food processor. Add the gelatin mixture and continue to blend for about 10 minutes, until the mixture has thickened and begun to cool. When cool, add the butter in batches, blending until fully combined. Transfer the crémeux to a plastic bowl, cover with plastic wrap so it touches the surface, and refrigerate until completely cool.

When you're ready to assemble the macarons, transfer the crémeux to a piping bag. Turn half the macarons over, flat sides up. Pipe the filling on the flat side of one of the macarons to cover. Sandwich with a second macaron, flat side in, like a sweet burger. Repeat with the remaining macaron shells and filling. Enjoy!

THE SWEET STUFF

BLOOD ORANGE MACARONS

MAKES AT LEAST 25 MACARONS

Blood oranges are my favorite type of citrus—I love their tartness and of course the color is amazing. Blood orange works especially well in macarons because this tartness cuts through the sweetness of the shell and makes the color of the macaron filling so striking. If blood oranges aren't available, choose mandarins or kumquats to replace the juice and zest; regular oranges will be too sweet.

INGREDIENT	WEIGHT	VOLUME
1 recipe Macaron Shells (page 152)	--------	--------
orange liquid food coloring (see Sources, page 250)	3 grams	1/2 teaspoon
Blood Orange Crémeux		
blood orange concentrate (see Sources, page 250)	400 grams	1 2/3 cups
3 sheets gelatin	6 grams	---------
3 1/2 large egg yolks	60 grams	3 tablespoons + 2 teaspoons
sugar	50 grams	1/4 cup
cornstarch	25 grams	3 tablespoons
zest and juice of 1 blood orange	--------	--------
unsalted European-style butter	250 grams	1 cup + 2 tablespoons

Prepare the macaron shells using the orange food coloring. Bake and let cool.

Make the crémeux: In a saucepan, heat the blood orange concentrate until just boiling. Soak the gelatin in cold water until soft; drain and squeeze out excess water.

In a large bowl, whisk together the egg yolks, sugar, and cornstarch. Pour the boiling purée over the egg mixture and return to the heat in a clean pan, whisking continuously until the mixture begins to boil. Immediately pour into a food processor. Add the drained gelatin and blend until it has thickened and cooled. When cool, add the orange zest and juice and butter and blend in the food processor until smooth.

Transfer the crémeux to a piping bag and reserve in the refrigerator until you're ready to assemble the macarons.

To assemble the macarons, turn half the macarons over, flat sides up. Pipe the filling on the flat side of one of the macarons to cover. Sandwich with a second macaron, flat side in. Repeat with the remaining macaron shells and filling.

SALTED CARAMEL MACARONS

MAKES AT LEAST 25 MACARONS

Salted caramel is almost a mainstay in pâtisseries nowadays—the sweet and salty combination has seduced us all, so it's no wonder this is always a best seller. The quality of vanilla and the correct type of flaky sea salt make a big difference here, so try to find the best quality available.

INGREDIENT	WEIGHT	VOLUME
1 recipe Macaron Shells (page 152)	--------	--------
brown liquid food coloring (see Sources, page 250)	4 grams	3/4 teaspoon
Salted Caramel		
heavy cream	400 grams	1 3/4 cups
1 Madagascar vanilla bean, split lengthwise, seeds scraped	--------	--------
fleur de sel	2.5 grams	1/2 teaspoon
sugar	300 grams	1 1/2 cups
glucose or corn syrup (see Sources, page 251)	100 grams	5 tablespoons
unsalted European-style butter	200 grams	14 tablespoons

Prepare the macaron shells using the brown food coloring. Bake and let cool.

In a saucepan, bring the cream, vanilla bean, and salt to a boil. Remove from the heat and reserve.

In a large pan over a medium heat, cook the sugar and glucose to a deep caramel. Deglaze the pan with three-quarters of the butter, then deglaze with the hot cream infusion.

Continue to cook until the caramel reaches 221°F on a Thermapen or candy thermometer. Add the remaining butter and blend with a hand blender or whisk until emulsified.

Cover with plastic wrap and cool in the refrigerator. Transfer to a piping bag and reserve until you're ready to assemble the macarons.

Pipe the salted caramel on the flat sides of half of the macaron shells and sandwich with the remaining half.

JASMINE TEA MACARONS
MAKES AT LEAST 25 MACARONS

Jasmine tea and chocolate are a dreamy combination: the tea is so floral—it really enhances the natural chocolate flavor. Here I have flavored both the filling and the shell to give it an extra kick. I always believe that you should be able to taste a dessert blindfolded and know what is in it. This recipe definitely passes the test.

TIP: After you have piped the macarons, sprinkle some tea leaves liberally over the shells before they dry out. The leaves will stick to the macarons and enhance the flavor, too.

INGREDIENT	WEIGHT	VOLUME
1 recipe Macaron Shells *(page 152)*	--------	--------
white liquid food coloring *(see Sources, page 250)*	3 grams	1/2 teaspoon
Jasmine Tea Ganache		
loose jasmine tea leaves, plus some more to garnish	20 grams	--------
heavy cream, plus a little more to top off	500 grams	2 cups + 2 1/2 tablespoons
Trimoline *(invert sugar)* or corn syrup *(see tip below)*	60 grams	2 1/2 tablespoons
dark semisweet chocolate, preferably Valrhona Manjari pistols or bars *(64% cacao; see Sources, page 250)*	450 grams	2 2/3 cups chopped, if using bars
unsalted European-style butter, softened	160 grams	11 tablespoons + 1 teaspoon

Prepare the macaron shells using the white food coloring. Bake and let cool.

Make the jasmine tea ganache: Put the loose tea in a saucepan, cover with a little water, and bring to a simmer, reducing the liquid until the tea is dry again. Immediately add the cream and allow it to heat but do not let it boil. Cover the pot and leave it to infuse for at least 30 minutes.

Strain through a fine-mesh sieve, reserving the tea leaves. Bring the cream back up to its original volume (500 grams) by adding some additional cream. Add the Trimoline and return the mixture to a boil.

TIP: Trimoline is an invert sugar that is commonly used in the professional pastry industry. If you cannot source it, liquid glucose (see Sources, page 251) or corn syrup can be substituted.

Place the chocolate in a large bowl and make a well in the middle. Pour the hot cream mixture into the chocolate in three stages, mixing in a clockwise direction with a spatula until a smooth and glossy ganache is achieved. Using a hand blender or whisk, mix in the butter until it is fully incorporated. Allow to set in the refrigerator.

Pipe the ganache on the flat sides of half of the macaron shells and sandwich with the remaining half.

BANANA-AND-LIME CARAMEL MACARONS
MAKES AT LEAST 25 MACARONS

Banana can be quite a difficult flavor to capture. Here, the addition of lime to the caramel enhances the banana flavor. Also, without the lime, the caramel is too sweet and a little boring—the fresh lime zest really brings it to life.

INGREDIENT	WEIGHT	VOLUME
1 recipe Macaron Shells (page 152)	--------	--------
yellow liquid food coloring (see Sources, page 250)	3 grams	1/2 teaspoon
green food powder (see Sources, page 250)	3 grams	1 teaspoon
Banana-and-Lime Caramel		
sugar	250 grams	1 1/4 cups
glucose or corn syrup (see Sources, page 251)	30 grams	4 1/4 teaspoons
water	75 grams	5 tablespoons
heavy cream, hot	200 grams	14 tablespoons
1 banana, diced	--------	--------
cocoa butter	20 grams	3 3/4 teaspoons
salt	6 grams	1 teaspoon
unsalted European-style butter	200 grams	14 tablespoons
banana purée (see Sources, page 250)	130 grams	2/3 cup
crème de banane (see Sources, page 250)	5 grams	1 teaspoon
zest of 2 limes	--------	--------

Prepare the macaron shells using the yellow food coloring. Bake and let cool.

Make the caramel: In a saucepan, bring the sugar, glucose, and water to a boil until an amber caramel is achieved.

Stir in the hot cream, then add the diced banana and reduce over a medium heat for 5 minutes. Whisk in the cocoa butter and salt, then whisk in the butter.

Off heat, stir in the banana purée, crème de banane, and lime zest. Allow to set in the refrigerator.

Transfer the caramel to a piping bag and reserve in the refrigerator until you're ready to assemble the macarons.

Pipe the ganache on the flat sides of half of the macaron shells and sandwich with the remaining half.

Dust the finished macarons with the green powder using a small paintbrush.

CHOCOLATE-HAZELNUT MACARONS
MAKES AT LEAST 25 MACARONS

A classic, and classics are classics for a reason—this flavor pairing is a timeless combination and a sure crowd-pleaser.

TIP: After you have piped these macarons, sprinkle the chopped hazelnuts liberally over the macarons before they dry out—this way the chopped nuts will stick to the macaron during the whole process—this gives the macarons a great flavor also.

INGREDIENT	WEIGHT	VOLUME
1 recipe Macaron Shells (page 152)	--------	--------
brown liquid food coloring (see Sources, page 250)	5 grams	1 teaspoon
hazelnuts, finely chopped, for finishing	100 grams	14 tablespoons
Hazelnut Ganache		
heavy cream	250 grams	1 cup + 1 tablespoon
praline paste	50 grams	3 tablespoons
gianduja (chocolate-hazelnut) spread (see Sources, page 250)	170 grams	9 tablespoons
semisweet dark chocolate, preferably Valrhona Noir Caraïbe pistoles or bars (66% cacao; see Sources, page 250)	50 grams	5 tablespoons chopped, if using chocolate bars
unsalted European-style butter, at room temperature	20 grams	1 1/2 tablespoons
glucose or corn syrup (see Sources, page 251)	35 grams	5 teaspoons
For Garnish		
gold powder and leaves, for finishing (optional)	5 grams	1 1/2 teaspoons

Prepare the macaron shells using the brown food coloring. Bake and let cool.

Make the hazelnut ganache: Bring the cream to a rapid boil with the glucose and praline paste.

Pour over the chocolate and butter, mix until the chocolate is melted and fully homogenized.

Transfer the ganache to a piping bag and reserve in the refrigerator until you're ready to assemble the macarons.

Pipe the ganache on the flat sides of half of the macaron shells and sandwich with the remaining half.

For a finishing touch, lightly dust with edible gold powder or gold leaves.

PB&J
MACARONS
MAKES AT LEAST 25 MACARONS

A bit of nostalgia, for the sophisticated child in all of us: this is the grown-up edition of PB&J—the sour cherry cuts through the richness of the peanut butter. These are fun and addictive.

TIP: *Make the full Sour Cherry Jam recipe, store it in the fridge, and try using it to fill the plain Kouign-Amann (page 58).*

Prepare the macaron shells using the purple food coloring. Sprinkle the shells with the chopped roasted peanuts immediately after piping. Bake and let cool.

Make the ganache: In a saucepan, bring the cream and Trimoline to a boil.

Place the chocolate in a large bowl and make a well in the middle. Pour the hot cream into the chocolate in three stages, mixing in a clockwise direction with a spatula until a smooth and glossy ganache is achieved.

Using a hand blender or whisk, mix in the butter and peanut butter until fully incorporated. Transfer the ganache to a piping bag and reserve in the refrigerator until you're ready to assemble the macarons.

Make the jam: In a large saucepan, bring the purée and 200 grams (1 cup) of the sugar to a boil over medium heat, whisking periodically.

In a separate bowl, combine the remaining 45 grams (scant 1/4 cup) of sugar with the pectin in a bowl and make sure to mix well.

Once boiling, add the pectin-sugar mix to the purée and whisk constantly until all is incorporated (2 to 3 minutes). Allow the mixture to simmer gently, stirring periodically to prevent it from burning, and bring the jam to 221°F—check the temperature using a Thermapen or candy thermometer. Remove from the heat, whisk in the cherry compound, and allow to cool before transferring to a piping bag.

To assemble the macarons, turn half of them over, flat sides up. Pipe a ring of peanut butter ganache around the inside edge of a macaron, on the flat side. Pipe the sour cherry jam to fill in the center of the ring. Sandwich with a second macaron, flat side in, like a sweet burger. Repeat with the remaining macaron shells, ganache, and jam.

INGREDIENT	WEIGHT	VOLUME
1 recipe Macaron Shells (page 152)	--------	--------
purple liquid food coloring (see Sources, page 250)	3 grams	1/2 teaspoon
chopped roasted peanuts	100 grams	3/4 cup
Peanut Butter Ganache		
heavy cream	250 grams	1 cup + 1 tablespoon
Trimoline (invert sugar) or corn syrup	30 grams	3 3/4 teaspoons
milk chocolate, preferably Valrhona Bahibé pistoles or bars (46% cacao; see Sources, page 250)	200 grams	1 cup + 3 tablespoons chopped, if using chocolate bars
unsalted European-style butter, softened	90 grams	6 tablespoons + 1 teaspoon
creamy organic peanut butter	130 grams	1/2 cup
salt to taste	-------	--------
Sour Cherry Jam		
cherry purée (see Sources, page 251)	500 grams	2 cups
sugar	245 grams	1 cup + 3 1/2 tablespoons
pectin (see Sources, page 251)	45 grams	5 tablespoons
sour cherry compound (see Sources, page 251)	150 grams or 1 3/4 ounces	7 1/2 tablespoons

CONFECTIONS

These are not your normal candy store sweets. Consisting of some elevated ideas of childhood memories, most of these confections may look complex but are quick and easy to make. One of my prized recipes is for the flavored caramels—inspired by a creation by Jacques Genin, whose patisserie is my favorite in Paris—which have just the right amount of softness and chewiness, making them incredibly delicious. The honeycomb crispies go well with pretty much everything, especially when broken up over ice cream. All of these confections will last for a long time if you store them in a sealed container to avoid any moisture getting to them, and, of course, if they don't get eaten first.

CARAMELS

MAKES FORTY 1/2 X 2-INCH CARAMELS

This recipe is inspired by Jacques Genin, a pastry chef based in Paris. It's worth taking a trip to the patisserie Jacques Genin just to taste his caramels, but everything else, such as his mille feuille and chocolates, are also exceptional. This recipe is all about the butter. I use French butter, lightly salted with a lower moisture content, to make a beurre noisette, also known as brown butter, because it creates a natural nutty flavor that ensures this recipe is not all about the sugar. These caramels should melt on your tongue, not stick to your teeth. I've included hazelnut and mango-passionfruit variations, but feel free to experiment with your own flavors—just be sure to go with something that balances the sweetness.

Line a half-sheet pan with parchment paper and spray the parchment with nonstick cooking spray.

In a deep saucepan, boil the butter until it separates and begins to color on the base of the pan. (This is beurre noisette.) Add the cream, glucose, and baking soda and return to a boil.

In another deep saucepan over a medium heat, dry caramelize the sugar for about 10 minutes, until a deep brown color is achieved.

Add the butter and cream mixture to the caramelized sugar and heat over a medium heat until it registers 241°F on a Thermapen or candy thermometer.

Pour the hot caramel on the prepared half-sheet pan and allow to set overnight in a cool place.

Using a long serrated knife, and working with just one-third of the pan at a time, cut the caramel into 2-inch strips, then cut each strip crosswise into 1/2-inch strips. Immediately wrap each individual caramel in a cellophane wrapper. Repeat the same process with the other two-thirds of the pan.

INGREDIENT	WEIGHT	VOLUME
lightly salted French butter, such as Beurre d'Isgny Demi-Sel (see Sources, page 250)	400 grams	1 3/4 cups
heavy cream	1 kilogram	4 1/3 cups
glucose or corn syrup (see Sources, page 251)	100 grams	5 tablespoons
baking soda	2 grams	1/2 teaspoon
sugar	750 grams	3 3/4 cups

TIP: The temperature here is vital: if it's 237 to 239°F, the caramel may be too soft; 244 to 246°F and, while still delicious, it may be too hard.

TIP: Don't cool these caramels in the fridge—moisture and sugar do not like each other. Instead put them somewhere cool where the sugar can recrystallize.

TIP: Once cut, the caramels must be wrapped immediately so they maintain their shape. This is why I've suggested that you cut and wrap them a third at a time. Cellophane wrappers are the best thing to use (see Sources, page 250), however, parchment paper cut into small squares works well, too. You may cut your caramels another size if you prefer; just be sure to create even strips so your caramels all end up the same size.

ADDITIONAL FLAVORS

HAZELNUT

Lightly roast 250 grams (2 1/2 cups) of hazelnuts in a preheated 300°F oven for 15 minutes until golden brown. Spread the toasted nuts evenly on the prepared half-sheet pan and pour the hot caramel over the nuts as evenly as possible. Allow to set and cut into pieces as described at left in the recipe for caramels.

MANGO-PASSIONFRUIT

Replace 200 grams (14 tablespoons) of the cream with 100 grams (6 tablespoons) of mango purée and 100 grams (6 1/2 tablespoons) of passionfruit purée (see Sources, page 251), then continue according to the recipe instructions for caramels at left.

MADAGASCAR VANILLA

Add 3 scraped vanilla pods—seeds only—to the cream and bring to a boil and follow the base recipe procedure.

TIP: Store the scraped pods in sugar, in an airtight container, after a few weeks you will have vanilla sugar, perfect sprinkled over fresh fruit.

SICILIAN PISTACHIO

Lightly roast 250 grams (1 3/4 cups) of Sicilian pistachios spread evenly on a half-sheet pan for 10 minutes at 300°F, then pour the cooked caramel over the nuts as evenly as possible and fill the pan. Allow to set and then cut into pieces.

WALNUT OR CASHEW

Lightly roast 250 grams (2 cups) of walnuts or 250 grams (1 2/3 cups) of cashews for 15 minutes at 325°F, spread evenly over the half-sheet pan, then pour cooked caramel over the top of the nuts and fill the pan. Allow to set and then cut into pieces.

RASPBERRY, PECAN, & CHOCOLATE TOFFEE

MAKES 15 PORTIONS

This crunchy toffee is one of my favorites and so simple—the raspberries and pecans ensure that it doesn't just taste like sugar. This stuff is addictive—you have been warned.

NOTE: You will need a Thermapen or candy thermometer and nonstick silicone baking mats.

In a large pot, combine the butter, sugar, water, and fine sea salt, and bring to a boil. Stirring continually, cook over medium heat until the toffee mixture reaches 295°F on your Thermapen or your candy thermometer.

Off heat, stir in the vanilla.

Immediately pour the toffee mixture on one large silicone baking mat or divide into half onto two smaller baking mats and, using a spatula, spread it as thinly as possible. Allow to set somewhere cool and with low humidity for at least 30 minutes.

Meanwhile, melt the chocolate over a deep saucepan of simmering water.

When the toffee has set, pour half the chocolate over one side of the toffee and, using an offset spatula, quickly spread it to completely cover the toffee. Sprinkle liberally with the chopped pecans, freeze-dried raspberries, and Maldon sea salt.

Place in the refrigerator for 10 minutes, until the chocolate has set. Remove from the fridge, flip the toffee over so you have the plain side facing you and coat with the remaining chocolate, then chill again.

Once both sides have set, smash the toffee into large pieces with a rolling pin and store in resealable plastic bags.

INGREDIENT	WEIGHT	VOLUME
unsalted European-style butter	450 grams	2 cups
sugar	450 grams	2 1/4 cups
water	90 grams	6 tablespoons
fine sea salt	9 grams	2 teaspoons
pure vanilla extract	15 grams	3 3/4 teaspoons
dark semisweet chocolate, preferably Valrhona Manjari pistoles or bars *(64% cacao; see Sources, page 250)*	500 grams	scant 3 cups chopped, if using chocolate bars
chopped pecans	25 grams	3 1/2 tablespoons
freeze-dried raspberries *(see Sources, page 250)*	50 grams	6 tablespoons
Maldon sea salt, for finishing	8 grams	1 1/2 teaspoons

THE SWEET STUFF

HONEYCOMB CRUNCHIES

MAKES 15 SERVINGS

This honeycomb candy is so simple and fun to make—three ingredients and about 5 minutes are all you need. It can be enjoyed on its own or sprinkled on top of your favorite ice cream for added flavor and crunch.

Line a half-sheet pan with parchment paper and spray it with nonstick cooking spray.

In a deep saucepan, bring the honey, golden syrup, sugar, and water to a boil. Continue to cook until a light caramel is achieved. Sift the baking soda and add it to the pot, whisking lightly.

Pour the caramel onto the parchment and allow it to cool and harden.

When completely cool, hit the caramel with a rolling pin to break it up into bite-size chunks, and store in resealable plastic bags.

INGREDIENT	WEIGHT	VOLUME
honey	30 grams	4 teaspoons
golden syrup	30 grams	4 1/4 teaspoons
sugar	180 grams	14 1/3 tablespoons
water	30 grams	2 tablespoons
baking soda	12 grams	2 1/2 teaspoons

SUNDAY BAKING

This chapter is called Sunday Baking because the recipes included here are perfect for times when you have a few spare hours and want to bake something fun and different. (Of course you don't have to do it on Sunday, any day will work!) Most of these recipes require sweet pastry; my suggestion would be to make a large batch of the pastry, then divide it into blocks and freeze them individually, so when the urge to bake takes over you, you're all ready to go. Just be sure to allow time for the pastry to thaw.

Happy baking!

PUFF
PASTRY
MAKES 2 HALF-SHEET PANS

Like the croissants, puff pastry is also made from a laminated dough. The method is exactly the same even though the dough and resulting pastry are slightly different; refer to the croissant dough explanation and step-by-step instructions for more detailed guidance. Puff pastry dough can also be made ahead then wrapped and stored in the freezer for up to three months.

INGREDIENT	WEIGHT	VOLUME
water	330 grams	1 cup + 6 1/3 tablespoons
fresh lemon juice	8 grams	1/2 tablespoon
bread flour, preferably King Arthur Special Patent	695 grams	5 1/3 cups
salt	16 grams	2 1/2 teaspoons
unsalted European-style butter, softened	70 grams	5 tablespoons
butter block (see page 32)	500 grams	2 1/4 cups

MIX
THE DOUGH

In a large mixing bowl, combine 90 percent of the water with the lemon juice. Add the flour, salt, and softened butter.

Transfer to a stand mixer with a dough hook attachment and mix on a low speed for 3 minutes. The dough will begin to come together but still be shaggy. Add the remaining water and continue to mix for 3 minutes more.

Place the dough on a half-sheet pan and shape into a rectangle. Cover with plastic wrap and store in the refrigerator for at least 1 hour and up to 3 hours.

LAMINATE
THE DOUGH

Place the butter block on plastic wrap. Hit the butter with the rolling pin so it flattens out into a rectangular shape, approximately 7 by 7 inches. Place in the refrigerator while you roll out the dough.

Transfer the dough to a floured surface and roll it out into a rectangle, approximately 10 by 9 inches.

Place the butter block in the middle of the 10 by 9 inch dough rectangle. Fold the sides of the dough over and into the center to cover the butter. Using your fingers, pinch together each side so the dough is completely sealed and no butter can be seen. (For additional help with this process, refer to the laminated dough steps on page 34.)

Rotate the dough 90 degrees clockwise and press down firmly onto the seams with a rolling pin, compressing evenly to lock in the butter on both sides.

Rotate the dough back to its original position and begin rolling it out lengthwise until the rectangle is approximately 5 by 14 inches.

Fold one third of the dough into the center and then fold the last third on top as if you were folding a letter. This is called a letter fold.

After the first fold, let the dough rest for 1 hour in the refrigerator.

After the first letter fold has rested, rotate the dough back to its original position and begin rolling it out lengthwise until the rectangle is approximately 5 by 14 inches.

Complete another letter fold and let the dough rest for 3 hours in the refrigerator.

For the third and last time, rotate the dough back to its original position and begin rolling it out lengthwise until the rectangle is approximately 5 by 14 inches. Complete the third letter fold.

After the third letter fold, let the dough rest overnight or for 8 to 10 hours.

RESHAPE
THE PASTRY

The dough is now laminated, relaxed, and cold.

Roll the dough out on a lightly floured surface to a thickness of 1/8 to 1/4 inch, maintaining its rectangular shape. The desired thickness is more important than the exact dimensions.

BAKE
THE PASTRY

Preheat the oven to 375°F. Line a half-sheet pan with parchment paper and then place the pastry in the pan. Cover the pastry with an additional sheet of parchment paper and then place a second half-sheet pan on top of the paper. Bake for 10 to 12 minutes, until the pastry is a deep golden brown. Allow to cool before cutting.

TIP: If the top half-sheet pan rises too far up as the pastry bakes, gently press down using oven gloves to release the excess steam; otherwise the air pockets in the dough will be too large and the pastry will flake when you try to cut it.

CHOCOLATE BABKA

MAKES 2 LOAVES

Babka is a historic bread that's made a huge comeback in recent years—and it's easy to see why it's so popular. Chocolate Babka is my interpretation of the classic.

This recipe calls for laminated dough. You can make a new batch, or use up leftover trimmings from making croissants or kouign-amanns if you've reserved some in the freezer. The ingredients will make two loaves, but feel free to create miniature babkas if you prefer (see the tip at the end of the recipe).

Melt the chocolate in a metal bowl over simmering water.

In a large bowl, whisk together the egg whites, confectioners' sugar, flour, and salt until well combined with no lumps.

Pour the melted chocolate into the egg white mixture, whisking continuously to keep the chocolate from seizing up, until well combined and lump free. Spoon the filling into a piping bag and reserve.

To assemble the babka, lightly flour a work surface with all-purpose flour. Using a rolling pin, roll out the laminated dough, rotating and moving it after each roll, until you have a 19 by 9-inch rectangle.

With a long side nearest to you, spread the chocolate filling over the dough as evenly as possible, leaving a 1-inch border all the way around the rectangle.

Starting with the long side near you, roll up the dough to form a long tube. You should see a spiral of dough and chocolate on the ends of the tube.

TIP: Roll the dough up very gently, so you don't push the filling out of the sides.

Using a serrated knife, cut the cylinder of dough crosswise into six 3-inch-wide slices.

Spray two 10-inch loaf pans with nonstick cooking spray. Place three of the dough slices in each pan, spirals facing upward. Cover with a plastic box and allow to proof somewhere warm for 2 hours. When the dough has risen just below the rim of the loaf pans, they're ready to bake.

Preheat the oven to 350°F. Bake the babkas for 30 to 40 minutes, until they are a deep golden brown.

INGREDIENT	WEIGHT	VOLUME
1 (12 x 9-inch) block laminated dough (page 32)	--------	--------
neutral glaze, for finishing (see Sources, page 250)	100 grams	1/3 cup
Chocolate Filling		
baking chocolate (see Sources, page 250)	250 grams (or 8 3/4 ounces)	1 1/2 cups
6 1/2 large egg whites	200 grams	13 tablespoons
confectioners' sugar	300 grams	2 2/3 cups
all-purpose flour, preferably King Arthur Sir Galahad artisan flour	40 grams	1/3 cup
salt	3 grams	1/2 teaspoon

TIP: To test if the loaves are done, insert a cake tester or small knife into the dough (the part without chocolate); if the blade comes out clean, the babkas are ready.

Turn out the loaves onto a wire rack to cool slightly before brushing the tops with neutral glaze to give them a great shine. The glaze will also help lock in the moisture.

TIP: If you prefer to make individual babkas as photographed overleaf, follow the process described above, but place each 3-inch slice upright in a 4-inch muffin tin and bake for 15 to 20 minutes, or until the mini babkas are a deep golden brown. This recipe will yield six mini babkas.

LEMON, YUZU, & MATCHA TART

MAKES ONE 10-INCH TART

In this reinvention of the classic tarte au citron, I've added the juice of a Japanese citrus fruit called yuzu, which has a much more floral flavor than lemon juice and makes the tart less acidic. However, if you can't get ahold of fresh yuzu, you can use lemon juice exclusively. A dusting of matcha—a brilliant green powdered tea—gives the tart an earthy flavor.

Make the lemon-yuzu filling: In a large bowl, whisk together the eggs and sugar. Whisk in the cream, followed by the yuzu juice and lemon juice and zest. Let infuse overnight in the refrigerator.

Make the sweet pastry dough: In a stand mixer with a beater attachment, cream together the butter and sugar until soft and pale. Slowly add the eggs, mixing until incorporated. Add the flour and mix together to form a paste.

Allow to rest in the refrigerator for at least 2 hours before using or wrap in a double layer of plastic and freeze until needed.

When you're ready to assemble and bake the tart, preheat the oven to 350°F.

Remove the pastry dough from the refrigerator and place it on a lightly floured work surface. Using a rolling pin, roll out the pastry into a disk no thicker than 1/2 centimeter. As you roll, rotate the dough occasionally and add additional flour as needed so it doesn't stick to the counter.

Roll the pastry up and around the rolling pin and then unroll it over the top of a 10-inch fluted tart pan that's 2 inches deep. Using your thumb and forefinger, gently press the dough into the base and sides of the pan; do not stretch the pastry. Using the rolling pin, roll over the top of the tart pan to remove any excess dough from the edges.

Line the inside of the tart shell with a 14-inch circle of parchment paper and fill the shell to the top with baking beans. Bake for 15 to 20 minutes, until lightly browned. Take the tart shell out of the oven and let it cool before removing the beans. Keep the oven on but reduce the oven temperature to 280°F.

Place the blind-baked tart shell on a half-sheet pan and transfer to the preheated oven. Strain the lemon-yuzu filling through a fine-mesh sieve and into a pitcher. Carefully pour the filling into the pastry in the oven. With this method, you avoid having to move the filled tart shell, and thus the risk of spills. Bake for 20 minutes, or just until the filling is set.

Allow the tart to cool, then remove it from the fluted ring and place on a plate. Dust the top with matcha powder and serve.

INGREDIENT	WEIGHT	VOLUME
Lemon-Yuzu Filling		
7 large eggs	330 grams	1 cup + 5 tablespoons
sugar	150 grams	3/4 cup
heavy cream	310 grams	1 1/3 cups
yuzu juice	42 grams	2 2/3 tablespoons
lemon juice	75 grams	4 3/4 tablespoons
zest of 2 lemons	--------	--------
Sweet Pastry		
unsalted European-style butter	340 grams	1 1/2 cups
sugar	225 grams	1 cup + 2 tablespoons
3 1/2 large eggs	180 grams	11 1/2 tablespoons
all-purpose flour, preferably King Arthur Sir Galahad artisan flour	675 grams	5 cups + 10 tablespoons
For Garnish		
Matcha powder, for dusting	--------	--------

TIP: Egg-based custards need to be cooked low and slow. This method stops the eggs from curdling, or getting a grainy eggy texture and flavor, instead creating a creamy smooth consistency and vibrant taste.

TIP: The consistency of the filling should be the same as Jell-O—set but still wobbly. If the custard ripples when you gently shake the pan, bake it longer, but remember that it will continue to cook once it's out of the oven.

PECAN PIE WITH ORANGE ZEST & SMOKED SALT

MAKES ONE 10-INCH TART

This dessert is a perfect choice for the holidays, but there's no reason not to serve it on other occasions. If you prefer a more classic version, feel free to leave out the orange zest and smoked salt.

Preheat the oven to 350°F.

Make the pecan filling: Using a stand mixer with the beater attachment, beat together the butter and demerara until soft and fluffy. Swap the beater for the whisk attachment and scrape down the sides of the bowl with a spatula. Whisking on a low speed, gradually stream in the eggs until fully incorporated. Add both syrups, the vanilla, orange zest, and smoked salt, whisking until well combined. Stop the mixer, remove the bowl, and use a wooden spoon to stir in the pecans.

TIP: Don't add the nuts to the stand mixer because the mechanical whisk might break them up.

Pour the pecan filling into the prebaked pastry shell. Place the pie on a half-sheet pan and transfer it to the middle rack of the preheated oven. Bake for 30 minutes, or until just set.

TIP: The consistency of the filling should be the same as Jell-O—set but still wobbly. If the mixture ripples when you gently shake the pan, bake it longer, but remember that it will continue to cook once it's out of the oven.

Allow the pie to cool to room temperature. Enjoy immediately or reserve in the fridge until ready to serve. Warm it up in a preheated 300°F oven before serving.

INGREDIENT	WEIGHT	VOLUME
1 prebaked 10-inch sweet pastry shell *(page 185)*	--------	--------
Pecan Filling		
unsalted European-style butter	75 grams	1/3 cup
demerara *(natural cane sugar)*	100 grams	1/2 cup
3 2/3 large eggs	180 grams	11 1/2 tablespoons
golden syrup *(see Sources, page 251)*	175 grams	1/2 cup
maple syrup	175 grams	generous 1/2 cup
pure vanilla extract	--------	1 teaspoon
zest of 2 oranges	--------	--------
smoked Maldon sea salt	10 grams	1 3/4 teaspoons
pecan halves	300 grams	3 cups

THE SWEET STUFF

LOCAL STRAWBERRY, VANILLA, BASIL, & BLACK PEPPER TART

MAKES ONE 10-INCH TART

Black pepper and strawberry may sound a little wacky, but trust me, it works. Try to get ahold of local strawberries when they are in season, either from a farmers' market or pick-your-own site. The ripe local berries are really the key to this dessert—let the ingredients speak for themselves.

INGREDIENT	WEIGHT	VOLUME
1 recipe Sweet Pastry Dough (page 185)	--------	--------
1 recipe Vanilla Pastry Cream (see right)	--------	3 cups + 5 tablespoons
freshly ground black pepper to taste	--------	--------
2 pints organic local strawberries, preferably wild	300 grams	2 cups
fresh basil leaves, preferably micro basil, for garnish	--------	--------

INGREDIENT	WEIGHT	VOLUME
Vanilla Pastry Cream		
milk	320 grams	1 1/3 cups
heavy cream	320 grams	1 cup + 6 tablespoons
salt	3 grams	1/2 teaspoon
sugar	160 grams	13 tablespoons
cornstarch	45 grams	1/3 cup
1 vanilla bean, split in half, seeds scraped	--------	--------
7 egg yolks	130 grams	1/2 cup
cold unsalted European-style butter, cut into cubes	80 grams	5 tablespoons + 2 teaspoons

Preheat the oven to 350°F.

On a lightly floured surface, roll out the sweet pastry dough until about 3 millimeters thick.

Using a rolling pin, roll up the pastry around the rolling pin, and then unroll it over the top of a 10-inch fluted cake ring. Using your thumb and forefinger, gently press the pastry into the bottom and sides of the cake ring. Roll the rolling pin over the top of the cake ring to cut off any excess pastry from the edges. Allow to rest in the refrigerator for at least 1 hour and up to 3 hours.

Line the inside of the tart shell with a 14-inch circle of parchment paper and fill to the top with baking beans. Bake in the middle of the oven for 20 minutes, until the pastry is a light golden brown. Allow to cool, then remove the baking beans and parchment paper.

Make the pastry cream: In a saucepan, whisk together the milk, cream, salt, and vanilla and bring to a boil. Mix together the sugar with the cornstarch until well combined. In a bowl, whisk the egg yolks together with the sugar and cornstarch mixture.

When the milk boils, slowly pour it over the egg mixture, whisking continually, then return it to the pot. Bring to a boil and whisk until the custard thickens. Reduce the heat and cook for another minute, whisking vigorously. At this stage it is very important that you do not stop whisking until the mixture has thickened; if you do the eggs may scramble.

Put the custard in the bowl of a stand mixer and whisk for 5 minutes, then add the cold butter and whisk until the custard has fully thickened. Pour it into a plastic container and cover with plastic wrap so it's touching the surface of the custard. Let cool in the refrigerator until needed.

Fill the pastry shell with the vanilla pastry cream until it reaches the top of the tart shell, smoothing it with a spatula so the surface is flat and smooth. Using a pepper mill, generously sprinkle black pepper on the pastry cream.

Trim off the tops of the strawberries and arrange them on top of the pastry cream. Garnish with the basil leaves and serve.

KUMQUAT-AND-HONEY RICE PUDDING

SERVES 8 TO 10

There is something about rice pudding that instantly takes me back to my childhood. When I was a kid we would typically eat rice pudding out of a can, and I still occasionally love to do that. This recipe is more refined, but it will still make you feel nostalgic. It is even better eaten cold the next day.

INGREDIENT	WEIGHT	VOLUME
risotto rice, such as arborio or baldo	360 grams	1 cup + 14 tablespoons
milk	-------	1 liter
heavy cream	-------	1 liter
sugar	320 grams	1 cup + 10 tablespoons
2 vanilla beans, split lengthwise, seeds scraped	--------	--------
egg yolks	300 grams	1 1/5 cups
1 recipe Poached Kumquats (see right)	--------	--------
Honeycomb Crunchies (page 175), for garnish	--------	--------

In a large saucepan, cook the rice with the milk, cream, 160 grams (13 tablespoons) of the sugar, and the scraped vanilla seeds (reserve the pods for another use). Bring to a simmer and cook for about 20 minutes, stirring occasionally to keep the rice from sticking to the bottom of the pan, until the rice is tender but still has a bite.

Whisk together the egg yolks and remaining 160 grams (13 tablespoons) of sugar in a bowl, add to the rice mixture, and cook over low heat, stirring constantly with a spatula, until the pudding has thickened.

TIP: At this stage, it is vital that you do not stop stirring; if you do the eggs could easily curdle. Always use a plastic spatula and avoid any metal utensils, as they will break up the rice, releasing the starch and making the rice pudding more stodgy than smooth.

Once thickened, pour the pudding onto a half-sheet pan or into a bowl to avoid overcooking, cover with plastic wrap so it is touching the surface of the pudding, and allow to cool.

Serve warm, room temperature, or chilled. (To reheat, warm a little milk in a saucepan with some of the leftover rice pudding.) To finish, garnish the pudding with some of the poached kumquats and honeycomb pieces—and enjoy immediately.

POACHED KUMQUATS

INGREDIENT	WEIGHT	VOLUME
kumquats	1.5 kilograms	--------
orange juice	--------	1 liter
water	--------	2 liters
sugar	1 kilogram	5 cups

Bring a saucepan of water to a boil.

Cut the kumquats in half, remove the seeds, and blanch in the boiling water 3 times, changing the water each time, to remove any bitterness.

In another pan, heat the 2 liters of water, the orange juice, and sugar over a medium heat, stirring until the sugar melts and a light syrup forms. Add the kumquats and slowly poach them until soft and tender, about 20 minutes. Reserve in a sealed container in the fridge, serve at room temperature.

THE SWEET STUFF

APPLE SPIRAL TART

MAKES ONE 10-INCH TART

This tart looks much more complicated than it really is—the spiral effect is actually very easy if you have the right tool. A vegetable turner is essential for the execution, and the result is well worth the expense. This recipe features a mix of cooked apple and fresh apple, which creates a nice texture. I recommend Fuji or Braeburn apples, but most varieties will work.

INGREDIENT	WEIGHT	VOLUME
12 Braeburn or Fuji apples	--------	--------
unsalted European-style butter	200 grams	14 tablespoons
sugar	200 grams	1 cup
1 recipe sweet pastry dough *(page 185)*	--------	--------
neutral glaze *(see Sources, page 250)*	50 grams	2 2/3 tablespoons
water	60 grams	1/4 cup

Peel, core, and chop 8 of the apples. Reserve the 4 other apples with peel intact.

In a heavy-bottomed pan, melt the butter with the sugar over medium heat and cook until lightly caramelized. Add the chopped apples to the caramel and stir to combine, cover with a lid, and cook for 15 to 20 minutes, stirring occasionally. Remove the lid, reduce the heat slightly, and continue to cook for approximately another hour until the apples have turned into a purée, reminiscent of apple butter, and a deep golden color has been achieved. We are looking for a dry, thick consistency.

While the apple and caramel filling is cooking, prepare the pastry shell. On a lightly floured surface, roll out the sweet pastry dough until it is about 1/8 inch thick. Roll up the pastry around the rolling pin, and then unroll it over the top of a 10-inch tart pan. Using your thumb and forefinger, gently press the pastry into the bottom and sides of the pan. Roll the rolling pin over the top of the pan to cut off any excess pastry from the edges. Allow to rest in the refrigerator for at least 1 hour and up to 3 hours.

When you're ready to bake the tart shell, preheat the oven to 350°F. Line the inside of the pastry with a 14-inch circle of parchment paper and then fill it to the top with baking beans. Bake in the middle of the oven for 20 minutes, until the pastry is a light golden color. Allow to cool, then remove the baking beans and parchment paper.

When the apple filling is ready, evenly spread it over the base of the cooked tart shell.

Using a vegetable turner, turn each of the remaining 4 apples to create thin strips. Once each apple is complete, using your hands roll the apple strips into a tight roll, adding more strips to the outside if any of the strips break. Cut the roll in half to create two spirals and place one spiral in the middle of the tart. Take the second spiral and wrap it tightly around the first spiral, skin side facing up. Repeat this process until the top of the tart is filled with one large, continuous apple spiral.

To finish, combine the neutral glaze with the water in a small saucepan and bring to a boil, whisking until there are no lumps. Using a pastry brush, liberally spread the glaze over the finished tart, and then allow to cool in the refrigerator until the glaze is set.

APPLE TARTE TATIN

MAKES FOUR 5-INCH TARTS

People always ask me "What's your favorite thing to bake?" and I always struggle with the answer because there isn't anything I dislike baking, otherwise I wouldn't bake it! The second most common question is "What's your favorite dessert to eat?" Again I struggle with my response. However, if I had to provide a single answer, apple tarte tatin would be my response to both questions.

This timeless dessert is brilliant in its simplicity, but you have to follow the rules. The recipe calls for just four ingredients—butter, sugar, puff pastry, and apples—but together they create an amazing flavor and texture that sums up everything I love about baking and eating.

Peel the apples and cut them into quarters and remove the core. Using a paring knife, bevel one edge of each quarter, then on the opposite side of the beveled edge, scoop out a curve with its deepest point at the center of the apple while keeping the edge. (This will allow the apple slices to slot into each other inside the pan and stay in place.) With the paring knife, round off the top and bottom of one apple quarter—this piece will be the center of each tart.

Using a pastry brush, generously coat the bottom of four 5-inch saucepans or skillets with one-quarter of the butter in each. (A copper saucepan is ideal, but not imperative.) Coat the butter with one-quarter of the sugar in each pan. Place the rounded pieces of apple in the middle of the buttered pans. Arrange 8 shaped apple slices inside each pan in a spiral around the central rounded apple, making sure each apple slots into the previous piece.

Cover the apples with a 6-inch puff pastry disc and make a couple of small holes in the middle of the puff pastry using the tip of a small knife, which will allow the steam to escape.

Preheat the oven to 360°F.

Place the tarte tatins over a gas or induction burner on a medium heat. When the sugar and butter begin to bubble and color slightly, forming a light caramel, transfer the pans to the oven and bake for about 40 minutes, until the puff pastry is browned and firm.

Turn the hot tarte tatins out onto a cooling rack. (Just give the base of the pan one strong tap and the tatin should release.) Serve immediately.

INGREDIENT	WEIGHT	VOLUME
9 Pink Lady apples (see Note below)	--------	--------
unsalted European-style butter, softened	250 grams	1 cup + 2 tablespoons
sugar	250 grams	1 1/4 cups
1 sheet unbaked puff pastry, cut into four 6-inch discs (page 178 or thaw before using if store-bought)	--------	--------

NOTE: *Pink Lady apples are essential to a successful tarte tatin. They have a lower water content than other varieties, which means they steam less as they bake, thus holding their shape and texture. Because they are drier, they also absorb more of the caramel.*

THE SWEET STUFF

RHUBARB & CUSTARD TART

MAKES ONE 10-INCH TART

Fish & chips and cups of tea aside, nothing is more quintessentially British than rhubarb and custard. Normally this would be presented as a rhubarb crumble with lumpy custard, the rhubarb picked from the garden, of course. This dessert is a bit more grown-up, but still nostalgic and very British!

Try to get organic free-range eggs for this recipe (and for all the recipes in this book, if possible); the custard will be much creamier and smoother, and the color will be a deep yellow, almost orange, rather than the practically white result you would get with regular store-bought eggs.

Poach the rhubarb: Pour the bottle of grenadine into a large pot. Fill the empty bottle with water and add it to the grenadine. Bring the poaching liquid to a boil.

Meanwhile, arrange the rhubarb in a long heat-proof container with a lid. Pour the boiling liquid over the rhubarb and shut the lid straightaway. Leave this to macerate overnight in the refrigerator.

When you're ready to make the vanilla custard, preheat the oven to 250°F.

In a saucepan, bring the cream, sugar, and vanilla seeds to a rapid boil.

Place the egg yolks in a bowl and pour the hot cream mixture over the yolks, stirring constantly until it's combined. Let stand for 5 minutes, then skim off any bubbles.

Pour the custard into the prebaked crust. Bake for 20 minutes, then rotate 180 degrees and cook for an additional 20 to 25 minutes, until the filling is set but still slightly wobbly.

Allow the custard tart to cool completely at room temperature, then place it in the fridge to prevent it from cracking.

Remove the rhubarb from the poaching liquid and drain it thoroughly on a clean kitchen towel. Using a paring knife, slice the rhubarb into 1/2-inch pieces, then arrange the rhubarb on top of the custard tart and serve.

INGREDIENT	WEIGHT	VOLUME
1 recipe prebaked Sweet Pastry Crust (page 185)	--------	--------
1 (16-ounce) bottle grenadine syrup	--------	--------
1 bunch red rhubarb, trimmed, washed, and cut in half	900 grams or 32 ounces	3 3/4 cups
Vanilla Custard		
heavy cream	500 grams	1/2 liter
sugar	110 grams	1/2 cup + 1 tablespoon
1 large vanilla bean, split lengthwise, seeds scraped	--------	--------
9 organic free-range egg yolks	170 grams	1/2 cup + 2 tablespoons

TIP: *Fun fact—when you rapidly boil the cream with the vanilla, the fat molecules in the cream will stick to the vanilla seeds and keep hold of them, so they'll be evenly distributed throughout the finished custard. Not only does this look more attractive, more importantly you'll enjoy vanilla flavor consistently, in every bite. (If you just warm up the mixture, the vanilla seeds will sink to the bottom and you'll get an overpowering vanilla flavor when you scoop up a bite near the base.)*

TIP: *The consistency of the filling should be the same as Jell-O—set but still wobbly. If the custard ripples when you gently shake the pan, bake it longer, but remember that it will continue to cook once it's out of the oven.*

TIP: *Egg-based custards need to be cooked low and slow. This method stops the eggs from curdling, or getting a grainy eggy texture and flavor, instead creating a creamy smooth consistency and vibrant taste.*

RASPBERRY & PISTACHIO TART

MAKES ONE 10-INCH TART

This recipe just says summer to me, and there is nothing better than picking your own berries, taking them home, and then making a beautiful tart or other fruit-driven dessert. The season is short, but if you can get your hands on local raspberries, the difference is amazing. If not, feel free to experiment with other types of berries local to you.

INGREDIENT	WEIGHT	VOLUME
1 recipe unbaked Sweet Pastry (page 185)	--------	--------
1 recipe Pistachio Pastry Cream (page 145)	--------	--------
4 pints organic raspberries	600 grams	8 cups
chopped pistachios	100 grams	3/4 cup
raspberry jam, for garnish	--------	--------

Preheat the oven to 350°F.

On a lightly floured surface, roll out the sweet pastry dough until about 3 millimeters thick. Using a rolling pin, roll up the pastry around the rolling pin, and then unroll it over the top of a 10-inch fluted tart pan. Using your thumb and forefinger, gently press the pastry into the bottom and sides of the pan. Roll the rolling pin over the top of the pan to cut off any excess pastry from the edges. Allow to rest in the refrigerator for at least 1 hour.

Line the inside of the tart shell with a 14-inch circle of parchment paper and fill to the top with baking beans. Bake in the middle of the oven for 20 minutes, until the pastry is a light golden color. Allow to cool, then remove the baking beans and parchment paper.

When the pastry is completely cool, use a spatula to spread the pistachio pastry cream into the tart crust, smoothing it around the edges so you end up with a flat surface all the way up to the rim of the pastry shell.

Starting next to the outside rim of the tart, make a circle with the raspberries, all facing up. Repeat the process until the tart is completely covered with raspberries.

For an added touch, using a piping bag, fill each raspberry with raspberry jam. Sprinkle with the chopped pistachios and serve.

COOKIES

It doesn't matter how old you are, people always love to have cookies. In this chapter I share a couple of classic recipes and a couple of classics reinvented, some savory, some sweet. All of these doughs can be made in a big batch and then frozen in smaller portions, so you can bake up a sheet of warm cookies whenever the need or mood strikes.

LEMON SHORTBREAD

MAKES 36 COOKIES

The lemon really livens up this classic shortbread. Use good quality European-style butter and you will taste the difference. Technique is important here, so follow the instructions and allow the cookies to cool long enough.

In a stand mixer using a paddle attachment, cream the butter, sugar, and lemon zest together until pale in color. Add the ground almonds and flour and mix until a dough forms.

On a lightly floured surface, roll out the dough until 1/2 inch thick. Using a 2 1/2-inch cookie cutter, cut out as many cookies as possible. Reroll the scraps and cut out the remaining cookies.

Transfer the cookies to a parchment paper–lined half-sheet pan. Prick the tops with a fork, sprinkle with a little sugar, and bake for 15 to 20 minutes, until lightly golden brown. Transfer to a wire rack to cool completely.

INGREDIENT	WEIGHT	VOLUME
unsalted European-style butter	375 grams	1 2/3 cups
sugar	190 grams	15 tablespoons
zest of 3 lemons	---------	--------
ground almonds	280 grams	3 cups
all-purpose flour, preferably King Arthur Sir Galahad artisan flour	280 grams	2 cups + 5 tablespoons

SNICKERS COOKIES

MAKES 30 SANDWICH COOKIES

Snickers was my favorite chocolate bar growing up. These cookies are a way to indulge in childhood nostalgia while still acting like an adult.

Preheat the oven to 350°F.

Toast the peanuts in a single layer in a shallow baking dish for 10 to 15 minutes, stirring once or twice and cooking until slightly underdone because the peanuts will continue to cook once removed from the oven. Allow to cool, then roughly chop. Leave the oven on.

Using a fine-mesh sieve, sift the flour, baking soda, and baking powder into a bowl.

In a stand mixer with a paddle attachment, cream together the butter and peanut butter until light and fluffy. Scrape the sides of the bowl with a spatula, add the brown sugar, and beat to incorporate. Scrape down the sides of the bowl again, turn the mixer on low speed, and add the egg. Mix in the vanilla. Add the flour mixture gradually, mixing for 30 seconds once it's all been added. Add the oats and chopped peanuts and mix until the dough just comes together.

Remove the dough from the bowl, wrap in plastic wrap, and allow to set in the fridge for 2 hours.

On a lightly floured surface, roll out the chilled dough until about 1/4 inch (1/2 cm) thick. Using a 4-inch cookie cutter, punch out as many cookies as possible. Reroll the scraps and cut out the remaining cookies.

Arrange the cookies on half-sheet pans lined with parchment paper. Bake for 10 to 12 minutes, until they are lightly golden brown. Transfer to a wire rack to cool completely.

When cool, fill a piping bag fitted with a 1/2-inch fluted tip with the peanut butter ganache. Turn half of the peanut cookies over so their bottoms face up. Pipe on a layer of the ganache and complete the sandwiches with a second cookie.

INGREDIENT	WEIGHT	VOLUME
unsalted peanut halves	30 grams	3 1/2 tablespoons
all-purpose flour, preferably King Arthur Sir Galahad artisan flour (see Sources, page 250)	200 grams	1 2/3 cups
baking soda	10 grams	2 teaspoons
baking powder	4 grams	scant 1 teaspoon
unsalted European-style butter, softened	210 grams	15 tablespoons
creamy peanut butter	90 grams	1/3 cup
light brown sugar	110 grams	1/2 cup packed
1 large egg	55 grams	3 1/2 tablespoons
pure vanilla extract	--------	1 teaspoon
rolled oats	110 grams	1 cup + 3 1/2 tablespoons
1/2 recipe Peanut Butter Ganache (page 167)	---------	--------

OAT & BLACK PEPPER COOKIES

MAKES 30 COOKIES

One word: cheese. Any cheese goes amazingly well with these cookies, which are more savory and spicy than sweet but irresistible nonetheless. Store in an airtight container and try to make them last for more than a day!

INGREDIENT	WEIGHT	VOLUME
unsalted European-style butter, softened	454 grams	2 cups
sugar	227 grams	1 cup + 2 tablespoons
all-purpose flour, preferably King Arthur Sir Galahad artisan flour (see Sources, page 250)	300 grams	2 1/2 cups
whole-wheat flour, preferably King Arthur brand (see Sources, page 250)	100 grams	3/4 cup
rolled oats	200 grams	2 1/4 cups
cracked black pepper	--------	1 tablespoon
salt	--------	1 tablespoon

Preheat the oven to 350°F.

In a stand mixer using a paddle attachment, cream together the butter and sugar. In a food processor, combine both flours and the oats and pulse until the oats are ground into a powder-like consistency. Stir in the cracked pepper and salt. Add the dry ingredients to the creamed butter and sugar in the mixer and mix until just incorporated. Transfer the dough to the refrigerator to chill for about 45 minutes.

On a lightly floured surface, roll out the chilled dough into a 1/2-inch-thick sheet. Transfer to a parchment paper–lined half-sheet pan and bake for 10 to 12 minutes, until lightly golden.

Using a 2 1/2-inch cookie cutter, punch out the cookies from the sheet of baked dough while it is still slightly warm. Transfer the cookies to a wire rack to cool completely.

MY OREO COOKIES

MAKES 36 COOKIES

These are very addictive: made with extra-dark cocoa powder and finished with flaky Maldon sea salt, they are a little bitter, a little salty, a little sweet, and very moreish.

INGREDIENT	WEIGHT	VOLUME
all-purpose flour, preferably King Arthur Sir Galahad artisan flour	480 grams	4 cups
extra brute cocoa powder (see Sources, page 250)	165 grams	1 1/4 cups
baking soda	3 grams	1/2 teaspoon
salt	6 grams	1 teaspoon
unsalted European-style butter	450 grams	2 cups
sugar	300 grams	1 1/2 cups
Maldon sea salt, for sprinkling	--------	--------
Vanilla Buttercream		
unsalted European-style butter	115 grams	1/2 cup
confectioners' sugar	240 grams	2 cups + 1 tablespoon
heavy cream	30 grams	2 tablespoons
vanilla extract	--------	1 teaspoon
salt to taste	--------	--------

Preheat the oven to 350°F.

In a medium bowl, whisk together the flour, cocoa powder, baking soda, and salt until evenly distributed. In a stand mixer using a paddle attachment, cream together the butter and sugar. Add the dry ingredients and mix until a dough forms.

On a lightly floured surface, roll out the dough until about 1/4 inch (1/2 cm) thick. Using a 2 1/2-inch fluted cookie cutter, punch out as many cookies as possible. Reroll the scraps and cut out the remaining cookies.

Transfer to parchment paper–lined half-sheet pans, prick the cookies with a fork, and sprinkle with Maldon sea salt. Bake for 8 to 10 minutes, then allow to cool for 5 minutes on the pans before transferring to a wire rack to cool completely.

Make the vanilla buttercream filling: Using a stand mixer with a beater attachment, beat the butter on a medium speed until it is soft and fluffy. Scrape down the sides of the bowl with a plastic spatula. Mix on a low speed, adding the confectioners' sugar, heavy cream, and vanilla extract, and continue to mix until there are no lumps. When finished, add salt to taste.

Place the buttercream in a sealed plastic container and store in the refrigerator for at least 1 hour before piping in between pairs of cookies. Buttercream will last in the fridge for at least least 3 weeks.

AFTER DARK

The beautiful thing about working with food, and pastry in particular, is the diversity. As you can see, just from the recipes contained in this book, the different skills and techniques required to prepare a wide repertoire of pastries and other baked goods means that there's always something new to learn, something new to try, and something new to achieve. Even as a professional, I will never get to a stage in my career when I know everything, and if I ever think I do, that means my career is over!

Why am I talking about this? This section, "After Dark," is not like the other sections in this cookbook. Many of the recipes contain multiple components, and some will call for a few ingredients that may be unfamiliar or new tools you may want to track down. (None of these items will break the bank; see Sources, pages 250–251.) The goal is not to intimidate; these recipes are designed to inspire you to try new things, enjoy the ride, and take pride in the results. Many are designed as dessert tasting plates, perfect for sharing, perhaps with a glass of bubbly.

I have served some of these recipes in fine dining establishments, but they can all be made in a home kitchen. If you don't have the molds or plates called for in a recipe, consider them a suggestion and try a glass or a plate you already have on hand. The flavor is the most important aspect to every recipe in this book; as long as you have that locked down, if your version doesn't look exactly like the ones in the photographs, it's totally fine. Be adventurous, try something different: once you know the rules, you can break them.

Although I love all the desserts I make, the recipes collected in this section are my favorites. The flavor combinations and execution push the envelope a little and some (like the boozy gummy bears) are just fun to make. And that's what baking should always be—fun! I hope you enjoy these recipes, this cookbook, and the results of your exploits in the kitchen!

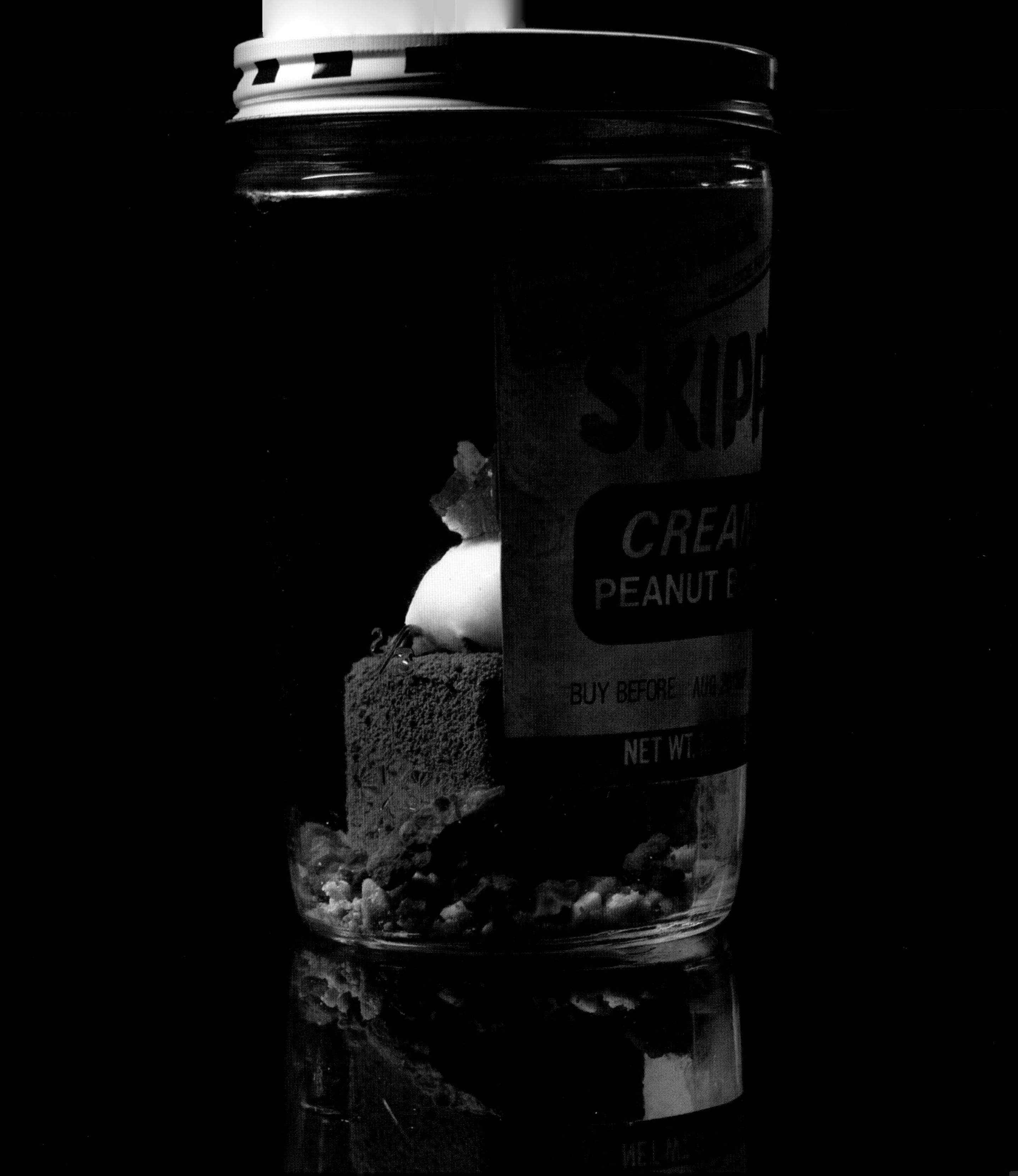
SKIPP
CREAM
PEANUT B
BUY BEFORE
NET WT.

PB&J

I serve this all-American classic in a vintage peanut butter jar to take you back to your childhood, when you ate the last bit out of the jar! Even though the ingredients for the mousse may sound heavy, the resulting dessert is light, balanced, and not too rich.

Soak the gelatin in cold water until soft; drain and squeeze out the excess water.

Put the sugar in a small saucepan and gradually add a small amount of water until the sugar resembles wet sand. Cook over medium heat until a sugar syrup forms and the temperature registers 245°F on a Thermapen.

Meanwhile, in a stand mixer with a whisk attachment, whip the yolks on high speed. Once the sugar reaches the desired temperature, turn down the mixer speed to low and gradually pour the sugar syrup onto the yolks, making sure the sugar does not touch the whisk, then return the speed to high. Add the drained gelatin to the egg mixture and whisk until the mixture has cooled and doubled in volume.

Turn the mixer off and add the peanut butter. Whisk again on a low speed until the peanut butter is incorporated, then pour into a separate bowl and reserve.

In the stand mixer with a clean whisk attachment and bowl, whip the cream almost to soft peaks. Using a spatula, fold the cream into the peanut butter mixture until the mousse is smooth and creamy and has no lumps.

Pipe the mousse into a silicone mold with small (approximately 1 1/4-inch) cubes or another mold of your choice and put in the freezer to set overnight.

The next day, melt the chocolate and cocoa butter together over a double boiler until smooth. Strain

INGREDIENT	WEIGHT	VOLUME
Peanut Butter Parfaits		
6 sheets gelatin	12 grams	--------
sugar	280 grams	1 cup + 6 1/2 tablespoons
15 large egg yolks	510 grams	2 cups
creamy organic peanut butter	170 grams	2/3 cup
heavy cream	1 kilogram	1 liter or 4 1/3 cups
Chocolate Coating		
semisweet dark chocolate, preferably Valrhona Noir Caraïbe pistoles or bars *(66% cacao; see Sources, page 250)*	700 grams	generous 4 cups chopped, if using chocolate bars
cocoa butter	300 grams	1 cup + 3 tablespoons
caramelized peanuts and freeze-dried raspberries, for sprinkling	--------	--------
banana-passionfruit sorbet *(see opposite page)*	--------	1 scoop per serving

through a fine-mesh sieve, allow to cool to room temperature before using.

Remove the cubes of frozen parfait squares from the mold and place them on a parchment-lined half-sheet pan. Fill a new paint sprayer with the dark chocolate coating and spray the frozen cubes to coat each side of the parfait then return to the freezer until ready to serve (see tip below). Leftover spray will keep covered in the refrigerator for up to 3 months.

TIP: To spray the chocolate coating onto the parfaits, you will need a new airbrush or paint sprayer (or one designated for culinary purposes only). Traditionally used to paint exteriors and other large surfaces, these are commonly found in hardware stores. This will give the parfaits a really fine covering of chocolate with a nice texture—just make sure the parfaits are frozen solid before spraying so they don't melt.

To assemble the PB&Js, place one peanut butter parfait in the base of each 16-ounce/pint mason jar. Sprinkle with some caramelized peanuts and freeze-dried raspberries. Top each serving with a quenelle of the banana-passionfruit sorbet.

BANANA-PASSIONFRUIT SORBET

MAKES 15 PORTIONS

INGREDIENT	WEIGHT	VOLUME
Sorbet Syrup		
Trimoline (invert sugar) or corn syrup	100 grams	1/4 cup
sugar	250 grams	1 1/4 cups
water	500 grams	2 cups + 2 tablespoons
Sorbet		
banana purée	500 grams	2 1/2 cups
passionfruit purée	75 grams	5 tablespoons
lemon juice	25 grams	5 teaspoons
Sorbet Syrup	470 grams	1 1/2 cups
(see recipe above)		

First make the sorbet syrup: In a small saucepan, combine the Trimoline, sugar, and water and bring to a boil over medium heat. Allow to cool before using.

Then make the sorbet: Combine both purées, the lemon juice, and sorbet syrup in an ice-cream machine and churn according to the manufacturer's instructions. This can take around 1 hour depending on the make and model of your machine.

MISO, PINK GRAPEFRUIT, & CASHEW

SERVES 15

This is an adventurous dessert, a great example of how traditionally savory ingredients can be used in desserts. The miso in the pudding is rich and intense and adds a strong savory umami flavor, but the pink grapefruit sorbet is sour and sweet and cuts through that, and the cashew cookie helps bring it all together. I like to serve this on a salt block, available at most home stores. Not only are they nice to look at, but as you eat off the block you get a little bit of salt in each bite, which helps balance the flavors in this dessert.

Soak the gelatin in cold water until soft; drain and squeeze out excess water.

In a medium-sized saucepan, heat the milk and cream over medium heat. Whisk in the brown sugar, salt, and toasted milk solids and continue to heat, whisking frequently, until the mixture boils and the sugar and milk solids are dissolved. Turn off the heat and whisk in the miso, butter, and drained gelatin.

Strain through a fine-mesh sieve into a mixing bowl. Allow the pudding to cool for 1 hour at room temperature before assembly.

To assemble the dessert, pour the miso pudding over the cashew cookie and chill in the refrigerator for at least 3 hours to set.

Cut the miso and cashew cookie into your desired shapes. Serve with the pink grapefruit sorbet, on a slab of pink Himalayan salt if possible.

INGREDIENT	WEIGHT	VOLUME
Miso Pudding		
6 sheets gelatin	12 grams	--------
milk	300 grams	1 1/4 cups
heavy cream	150 grams	2/3 cup
dark brown sugar	200 grams	13 1/2 tablespoons
salt	6.7 grams	1 teaspoon
toasted dry milk solids	100 grams	13 tablespoons
(toasted powdered milk works fine also—just be careful not to burn it)		
white miso paste	75 grams	4 1/2 tablespoons
cold unsalted European-style butter, cut into cubes	50 grams	3 1/2 tablespoons
1 recipe Cashew Cookie (see opposite page)	--------	1 cookie per serving
Pink Grapefruit Sorbet (see opposite page), for serving	--------	1 scoop per serving

CASHEW
COOKIE

INGREDIENT	WEIGHT	VOLUME
1 large egg	50 grams	3 tablespoons + 1/2 teaspoon
light brown sugar	200 grams	14 1/2 tablespoons
cashew butter	270 grams	1 cup + 1 tablespoon
baking soda	3 grams	1/2 teaspoon
chopped cashews	65 grams	1/2 cup
ground ginger	--------	1/2 teaspoon

Preheat the oven to 350°F.

In a food processor, mix all the ingredients until just combined; be sure not to overmix.

Press the dough into a half-sheet pan lined with parchment paper to create an even layer. Bake for 11 to 13 minutes, or until golden brown on top. Allow to cool on a wire rack.

PINK GRAPEFRUIT
SORBET

MAKES 15 PORTIONS

INGREDIENT	WEIGHT	VOLUME
pink grapefruit juice	1 kilogram	4 cups
sorbet stabilizer, such as Cremodan 64 (see Sources, page 251)	100 grams	generous 1/2 cup
Sorbet Syrup (see page 215)	400 grams	1 1/3 cups

Pour the grapefruit juice into a large bowl. In a medium-sized pot, combine the sorbet stabilizer and sorbet syrup and bring to a boil.

Pour the boiling syrup over the grapefruit juice and then chill over an ice bath.

When cold, strain through a fine-mesh sieve and churn in an ice-cream maker according to the manufacturer's instructions. Store in the freezer until serving time.

YUZU, HONEY, & PEARL BARLEY

MAKES 10 SERVINGS

I created this dish because of the respect I have for our very own NYC Rooftop Honey. Support local honey production wherever you can; without it we have nothing. This yuzu and honey parfait served with a scoop of an interesting pearl barley gelato is one of my favorite desserts: it offers great textures and contrasting flavors, yet it's simple and enjoyable.

Soak the gelatin sheet in cold water until soft; drain and squeeze out excess water.

In a small saucepan, heat the honey, sugar, and water over medium heat until it reaches 245°F on a Thermapen.

Meanwhile, in a stand mixer with a whisk attachment, begin whipping the egg and yolks together on high speed. Once the sugar reaches the desired temperature, turn down the mixer speed to low and gradually pour the sugar syrup onto the eggs, making sure the sugar does not touch the whisk.

Add the drained gelatin and whip the mixture on a high speed until full volume has been achieved or it has doubled in size. Lower the speed and gradually add the mango purée and yuzu juice until combined. Pour the custard mixture into a separate bowl and reserve.

In the stand mixer with a clean whip attachment, pour the cream into a clean bowl and whip to almost a soft peak. Using a spatula, fold the cream into the reserved egg mixture, ensuring that there are no lumps but being careful not to overmix and knock all the air out. (If this happens you will end up with a dense mousse, not a light and airy one.)

Pipe into quenelle-shaped molds (or other small molds) and let set for at lest 3 to 4 hours. In the freezer. Take off the mold while still frozen, to keep the shape.

To assemble the desserts, place each yuzu parfait, off center on a dessert plate, and allow 5 to 6 minutes to defrost before serving. Garnish the plates with dots of local honey, honeycomb crispies, and small quenelles of the pearl barley gelato. Sprinkle over some bee pollen to finish.

INGREDIENT	WEIGHT	VOLUME
Yuzu and Honey Parfaits		
1 sheet gelatin	2 grams	--------
honey	20 grams	2 3/4 teaspoons
sugar	25 grams	2 tablespoons
water	15 grams	3 teaspoons
1/2 large egg	25 grams	4 3/4 teaspoons
2 large egg yolks	40 grams	2 1/2 tablespoons
mango purée	150 grams	9 2/3 tablespoons
yuzu juice	32 grams	2 tablespoons
heavy cream	160 grams	11 tablespoons
1/2 recipe Pearl Barley Gelato (see opposite page)	--------	1 scoop per serving
Local honey, for drizzling	--------	--------
Honeycomb Crispies (recipe on page 175)	--------	--------
Bee pollen, for sprinkling	--------	--------

PEARL BARLEY GELATO

MAKES 20 PORTIONS

INGREDIENT	WEIGHT	VOLUME
milk	500 grams	2 cups + 1 tablespoon
sugar	100 grams	1/2 cup
glucose or corn syrup *(see Sources, page 251)*	40 grams	2 tablespoons
1/2 vanilla bean, pod and seeds	--------	--------
salt	6.7 grams	1 teaspoon
pearl barley	125 grams	10 tablespoons

In a medium-sized saucepan, combine the milk, sugar, glucose, vanilla seeds, and salt and bring to a boil. Stir in the barley, cook for 10 minutes, then remove from the heat and let steep for 30 minutes.

Chill over an ice bath until completely cool and strain through a fine-mesh sieve. Churn in an ice-cream maker according to the manufacturer's instructions.

BRILLAT SAVARIN & PASSIONFRUIT HUSK

MAKES 10 SERVINGS

This creamy cheesecake, made with a mix of cream cheese and Brillat Savarin (Brillat Savarin is a triple crème cheese, similar to brie but with a much more intense flavor), is a marriage between a cheese course and dessert. Passionfruits are expensive, so why waste any part of them? For this recipe, I scoop out the inside of the passionfruit (keep the pulp and seeds for the glaze and garnish), then fill the husks with the cheesecake. It makes for an attractive presentation, and the cheesecake also picks up a strong passionfruit flavor if you allow it to chill for 24 hours.

Soak eight gelatin sheets in cold water until soft.

In a stand mixer with a beater attachment, paddle the cream cheese and Brillat Savarin cheese until there are no lumps. Add the cream in stages, then the sugar, and continue paddling until the mixture is light and fluffy.

In a separate bowl, whisk the yolks until they reach the ribbon stage. Add the yolks to the creamy cheese mixture and mix to combine.

In a small saucepan, warm the Frangelico. Squeeze out the excess water from the gelatin and melt the gelatin in the Frangelico.

With the mixer on a low speed, stream the Frangelico into the creamy cheese mixture.

Strain the cheesecake filling through a fine-mesh sieve. Divide the filling among the empty passionfruit husks. Allow to set for at least 2 to 3 hours in the refrigerator (but preferably 24 hours).

Meanwhile make the passionfruit glaze: Soak six gelatin sheets in iced water until softened. Take the reserved passionfruit pulp and strain through a fine mesh sieve. Reserve the seeds.

In a small saucepan, heat the passionfruit juice over a low flame. Remove it from the heat just before the juice begins to boil. Using your hands, squeeze out the excess water from the gelatin and add it to the hot juice. Whisk until completely dissolved. Pass through a fine-mesh sieve and allow to cool at room temperature.

To clean the passionfruit seeds, put them in a medium-sized saucepan covered with water and boil for at least 30 minutes. Strain and wash through a fine-mesh sieve.

INGREDIENT	WEIGHT	VOLUME
Brillat Savarin		
Passionfruit Cheesecake		
8 sheets gelatin	16 grams	--------
cream cheese	200 grams	12 1/2 tablespoons
Brillat Savarin cheese	300 grams or 10 1/2 ounces	--------
heavy cream	500 grams	2 cups + 2 tablespoons
sugar	120 grams	9 1/2 tablespoons
10 egg yolks	180 grams	11 tablespoons
Frangelico hazelnut liqueur	150 grams	10 tablespoons
5 ripe passionfruits, cut in half, pulp reserved for glaze, seeds reserved for garnish	--------	--------
Passionfruit Glaze		
passionfruit pulp	250 grams	1 cup
6 sheets gelatin	12 grams	--------
For Garnish		
passionfruit seeds	--------	--------
edible pansies	--------	--------
micro cilantro	--------	--------

Once the cheesecake has set, remove the passionfruit halves from the fridge and pour a little of the room-temperature passionfruit glaze on top of the cheesecake until the tops are completely covered, around half a tablespoon of glaze per passionfruit half. Place them back in the refrigerator for at least one hour or until the glaze has set.

Garnish with the cleaned passionfruit seeds, edible pansies, and micro cilantro.

MEYER LEMON, CONCORD GRAPE, & POPPY SEED TUILE

MAKES ONE 12-INCH TART

I love this flavor combination. Concord grape at its peak is one of my favorite flavors: it has its own unique flavor nothing like a normal grape, while Meyer lemon has a much more floral taste than regular lemon. The window to get these ingredients is short, but that only makes this lemon tart with grape sorbet that much more enjoyable.

INGREDIENT	WEIGHT	VOLUME
Lemon Tart Filling		
11 large eggs	550 grams	2 cups + 3 tablespoons
sugar	300 grams	1 1/2 cups
heavy cream	396 grams	1 2/3 cups
fresh lemon juice	125 grams	1/2 cup
fresh Meyer lemon juice	125 grams	1/2 cup
zest of 2 lemons	--------	--------
1 prebaked 12-inch Pâte Brisée tart shell (recipe follows)	--------	--------
confectioners' sugar, for serving	--------	--------
Concord Grape Sorbet (recipe follows), for serving	--------	1 scoop per serving
Lemon Poppy Seed Tuiles (recipe follows), for serving	--------	1 tuile per serving

In a medium bowl, whisk together the eggs and sugar. Whisk in the cream followed by the lemon juice and the zest. Cover the bowl and put in the refrigerator to infuse overnight.

Assemble and bake the pâte brisée tart shell (see right). When you're ready to continue the recipe preheat the oven to 265°F.

Pass the lemon filling through a fine-mesh sieve and pour it into the 12-inch tart shell. Bake for 15 to 20 minutes, until the filling is just set. Chill in the refrigerator for at least 2 or 3 hours before cutting.

When you're ready to assemble the dessert, cut the lemon tart into the desired number of slices and lightly dust it with confectioners' sugar. If you like, use a blowtorch to lightly glaze the top until the sugar has caramelized. Serve each slice with a large scoop of the Concord grape sorbet—directly on top of the tart—and a tuile.

PÂTE BRISÉE

MAKES ENOUGH DOUGH FOR ONE 12-INCH TART

INGREDIENT	WEIGHT	VOLUME
all-purpose flour	500 grams	4 cups + 2 tablespoons
salt	11 grams	1 3/4 teaspoons
cold unsalted European-style butter, cut into cubes	260 grams	1 cup + 2 1/2 tablespoons
ice water	118 grams	1/2 cup
1 1/4 large eggs	60 grams	1/4 cup

In a stand mixer with a dough hook, combine the flour and salt. Add the cubed butter and mix until a fine crumb is achieved; do not overmix. Add the ice water and eggs and mix until just combined.

Remove the dough to a floured work surface and gently knead it, being careful not to overwork the dough. Wrap the dough tightly in plastic wrap and allow it to rest in the fridge for at least 3 hours, but preferably 24 hours.

When you're ready to bake the tart shell, preheat the oven to 350°F.

On a lightly floured work surface, roll out all of the pastry into a disc that's about 1/8 inch thick. Roll the disc onto the rolling pin, then unroll it gently over a 12-inch ring mold. Using your thumbs and forefingers, gently press the dough into the sides of the ring, then roll over the top of the ring mold to remove any excess dough. Line with parchment paper, and then fill with baking beans.

Bake for 20 minutes, or until the pastry is lightly golden brown.

Allow to cool then remove the parchment paper and baking beans.

CONCORD GRAPE SORBET

MAKES 20 PORTIONS

INGREDIENT	WEIGHT	VOLUME
1 recipe fresh Concord grape jam, from about 5 pounds grapes	--------	1 liter
Sorbet Syrup (page 215)	400 grams	2 cups
sorbet stabilizer, such as Cremodan 64 (see Sources, page 251)	100 grams	8 tablespoons

Create the Concord grape jam according to the recipe on page 71.

In a small saucepan, bring the sorbet syrup and stabilizer to a boil. Let cool over an ice bath, then mix them into the jam.

Transfer to an ice-cream maker and churn according to the manufacturer's instructions. Store in the freezer until ready to serve.

LEMON POPPY SEED TUILES

MAKES 10 TO 15 TUILES

INGREDIENT	WEIGHT	VOLUME
light brown sugar	100 grams	7 1/4 tablespoons
granulated sugar	100 grams	1/2 cup
all-purpose flour, preferably King Arthur Sir Galahad flour (see Sources, page 250)	100 grams	14 tablespoons
freshly squeezed lemon juice	100 grams	6 1/2 tablespoons
unsalted European-style butter, at room temperature, cut into cubes	100 grams	7 tablespoons
poppy seeds	25 grams	8 teaspoons

Put both sugars and the flour in a food processor. With the motor on, gradually pour in the lemon juice until well blended. Add the butter and pulse just until there are no more lumps.

Transfer the batter to a bowl, cover with plastic wrap, and chill in the refrigerator for at least 6 hours before using. (It can be stored in the fridge for up to 1 week, or wrapped in plastic wrap and frozen for up to 3 months.)

Preheat the oven to 350°F. Line a half-sheet pan with a silicone mat.

Scoop tablespoons of the batter onto the prepared half-sheet pan, spread each to form a thin round (make sure they don't touch), and then sprinkle with poppy seeds. Bake until a deep golden brown color, about 5 to 6 minutes. Allow to cool completely on the half-sheet pan.

COFFEE & LEMON

MAKES 10 SERVINGS

Espresso with lemon zest is a typical Italian drink—a classic Italian flavor combination and my inspiration for this dessert, which layers a coffee cream and salted chocolate ganache with lemon sorbet to contrast with the richness.

INGREDIENT	WEIGHT	VOLUME
Coffee Crémeux		
1 sheet gelatin	2 grams	--------
milk	150 grams	10 tablespoons
heavy cream, plus more as needed to rescale	150 grams	2/3 cup
coffee beans	65 grams	3 tablespoons
4 large egg yolks	75 grams	4 tablespoons + 2 teaspoons
sugar	32 grams	2 1/2 tablespoons
milk chocolate, preferably Valrhona Jivara Lactee pistoles or bars (see Sources, page 250)	125 grams	3/4 cup chopped, if using chocolate bars
cocoa butter	11 grams	2 teaspoons
cold unsalted European-style butter, cut into cubes	50 grams	3 1/2 tablespoons

Soak the gelatin leaves in cold water until soft; drain and squeeze out excess water.

In a small saucepan, heat the milk, cream, and coffee beans until just simmering, then remove from the heat, cover with plastic wrap, and let steep for 30 minutes. Strain into a bowl and rescale, adding additional cream to take the total weight back up to 300 grams (or about 1 1/3 cups). Transfer the coffee cream mixture to a small clean saucepan and bring to a simmer.

In a bowl, whisk together the egg yolks and sugar. Gradually add the hot coffee mixture, whisking constantly, to form custard. Transfer the custard to a clean medium-sized pan over medium heat and, using a spatula to mix constantly in a figure eight motion, cook until slightly thickened. Remove from the heat and stir in the drained gelatin.

Put the chocolate and cocoa butter in a large bowl. Using a fine-mesh sieve, strain the hot custard over the chocolate and cocoa butter. Using a hand blender, blend the hot custard, chocolate, and cocoa butter together until smooth and glossy. Add the unsalted butter and continue to blend until the butters are emulsified.

Allow to cool slightly. Pour the crémeux into 3-inch disc molds, or small molds of your choice, and freeze until serving time. Meanwhile, make the ganache and sherbet.

INGREDIENT	WEIGHT	VOLUME
Coffee Ganache		
heavy cream, plus more as needed	300 grams	1 1/4 cups
coffee beans	60 grams	scant 3 tablespoons
milk chocolate, preferably Valrhona Bahibé pistoles or bars (46% cacao; see Sources, page 250)	75 grams	7 tablespoons chopped, if using chocolate bars
dark semisweet chocolate, preferably Valrhona Manjari (64% cacao; see Sources, page 250)	125 grams	3/4 cups chopped, if using chocolate bars
glucose or corn syrup (see Sources, page 251)	35 grams	5 teaspoons
cold unsalted European-style butter, cut into cubes	20 grams	4 1/4 teaspoons

In a small saucepan, heat the cream and coffee beans until just simmering, remove from the heat, cover the pan with plastic wrap, and let steep for 30 minutes. Strain and rescale, adding additional cream to take the total weight back up to 300 grams (or about 1 1/4 cups).

Put both chocolates in a large bowl. Put the coffee cream in a small clean saucepan, add the glucose, and bring to a boil. Pour the coffee cream over the two chocolates and blend with a hand blender. When the ganache mixture is smooth and glossy, add the cubed butter, and continue to blend until the butter has been emulsified.

Pour the ganache into additional 3-inch disc molds, or small molds of your choice, and freeze until needed. Meanwhile, make the sherbet.

LEMON SHERBET SORBET

MAKES 20 PORTIONS

INGREDIENT	WEIGHT	VOLUME
heavy cream	160 grams	11 tablespoons
milk	500 grams	2 cups + 1 tablespoon
freshly squeezed lemon juice	320 grams	1 cup + 4 1/2 tablespoons
zest of 3 lemons	--------	-------
Sorbet Syrup (page 215)	400 grams	1 1/3 cups
sorbet stabilizer, such as Cremodan 64 (see Sources, page 251)	200 grams	1 cup + 2 teaspoons

Using a hand blender, blend together all the ingredients in a medium bowl. Transfer to an ice-cream maker and churn according to the manufacturer's instructions. Place in the freezer until ready to use.

When you're ready to assemble the desserts, remove the frozen crémeux and ganache discs from the freezer. Place the crémeux disc on top of the ganache disc in the middle of a small plate, and top with a small quenelle of lemon sherbet. Repeat to make 10 servings total. Serve immediately.

CONCORD GRAPE PARFAIT

SERVES 6

Concord grape season is very short—typically from October to January—so if you can find them, buy a bunch or more and process and freeze them. Both the smell and the flavor are unbelievable. This dessert includes two new ways to use this special harvest: in a parfait and in edible spheres.

To begin, prepare one recipe of Concord grape jam, following the instructions provided on page 71.

INGREDIENT	WEIGHT	VOLUME
Concord Grape Parfait		
1 1/2 sheets gelatin	3 grams	--------
sugar	45 gram	3 tablespoons + 2 teaspoons
honey	40 grams	2 tablespoons
water	30 grams	2 tablespoons
1 large egg	50 grams	3 tablespoons + 1 teaspoon
4 large egg yolks	80 grams	5 tablespoons
heavy cream	250 grams	1 cup + 1 tablespoon
1 recipe Concord grape jam *(see page 71)*	300 grams	1 1/3 cups
fresh lemon juice	42.5 grams	2 tablespoons + 2 teaspoons

Soak the gelatin in cold water until soft; drain and squeeze out excess water.

In a small saucepan, heat the sugar, honey, and water until a syrup forms and registers 245°F on a Thermapen.

In a stand mixer with a whisk attachment, whip the egg and yolks together on high speed. While whisking, gradually pour the sugar syrup over the egg mixture to create a pâte à bombe (see page 124 for instructions). Add the drained gelatin and continue to whip until the mixture reaches full volume.

Using a stand mixer with a clean whisk attachment, whip the cream in a separate bowl until it reaches soft peaks.

Add the Concord grape jam to the egg mixture and mix to combine.

Using a spatula, gently fold the grape mixture into the whipped cream and then incorporate the lemon juice.

Pour the parfait into two 8-inch ring molds with 6-inch molds sitting inside of them, all lined with acetate, and freeze for at least 4 hours. When the parfaits have set solid, remove the ring molds and acetate and cut each ring into three equal servings. (For ring molds, see Sources on page 251. Or feel free to use other molds that you have on hand for this dessert.)

INGREDIENT	WEIGHT	VOLUME
Concord Grape Spheres		
Concord grape jam	200 grams	about 1 cup
simple syrup *(1:1 ratio of sugar to water)*	7.5 grams	1/2 tablespoon
calcium lactate gluconate *(see Sources, page 251)*	2 grams	1/2 teaspoon
sodium alginate *(see Sources, page 251)*	5 grams	2 1/2 teaspoons
distilled water	1 kilogram	1 liter
store-bought Concord grape juice, for serving	--------	2 cups

In a small bowl, combine the grape jam, simple syrup, and calcium lactate gluconate, stirring well. Transfer the grape mixture to half-sphere molds that are 1 inch in diameter and put them in the freezer until frozen solid.

In a medium bowl, blend the sodium alginate with the water to create a sodium bath. Allow to rest for at least 1 hour.

Take the molds off the frozen spheres and place them in the sodium bath until a skin forms around each sphere. Remove and store the spheres in Concord grape juice. Place the sphere next to the parfait; either pop the sphere and eat it with the parfait or enjoy it in a single bite.

G & T

MAKES 20 SPHERES

Ready to show off? Whip up these gin-and-tonic-flavored spheres. The calcium lactate gluconate and sodium alginate are easily found online and are relatively easy to use: The process is called reverse spherification. It requires some patience, but it's well worth the effort, and you can use it to create multiple flavors.

In a small bowl, combine the gin, tonic, lime juice, simple syrup, and calcium lactate in a bowl, stirring well. Transfer the mixture into half-sphere molds that are 1 inch in diameter and put them in the freezer until frozen solid.

In a medium bowl, blend the sodium alginate with the water to create a sodium bath.

Take the molds off the spheres and place them in the sodium bath until a skin forms around each sphere. Remove and reserve in a small container filled with tonic water, and store in the refrigerator.

Serve the spheres on a teaspoon and eat them in one bite. They will have a very fine skin around them that will pop as soon as you bite into them.

INGREDIENT	WEIGHT	VOLUME
gin	--------	1 ounce
tonic	--------	1 ounce
fresh lime juice	--------	1/2 fluid ounce or 1 tablespoon
simple syrup *(1:1 ratio of sugar to water)*	--------	1/4 fluid ounce or 1/2 tablespoon
calcium lactate gluconate *(see Sources, page 251)*	--------	1/4 teaspoon
distilled water	1 kilogram	1 liter
sodium alginate *(see Sources, page 251)*	5 grams	2 1/2 teaspoons

EVOO & EUCALYPTUS

MAKES 3 PINTS

This is a great dessert for anyone who says they "don't like sweets." The gelato combines the best of both worlds, sweet and savory, while the minty, piney scent of eucalyptus (with just a touch of honey) enhances the sensory experience. Choose a high-quality olive oil, with a mild flavor.

Bring the water and Trimoline to a boil in a medium saucepan. In a bowl, combine the sugar, ice cream stabilizer, powdered milk, and dextrose and add to the boiling water, whisking constantly until the gelato base begins to expand. Remove from the heat and stream in the olive oil, whisking until the oil is emulsified. Whisk in the lemon juice and zest. Chill over an ice bath. Strain. Place in an ice cream maker/machine, churn until ice cream consistency, and store in the freezer until ready to serve.

To assemble the dessert, place some fresh eucalyptus leaves in a large serving bowl for each person, place a smaller bowl on top, and scoop the olive oil gelato into it. Finish with a drizzle of olive oil, a pinch of Maldon sea salt, and fresh lemon zest, then pour liquid nitrogen over the eucalyptus leaves to release the natural aroma and serve. The idea is that your guests will smell the eucalyptus before they taste the gelato, and when they do take that first bite, the combination of both the fragrance and taste will affect the final flavor.

INGREDIENT	WEIGHT	VOLUME
Olive Oil Gelato		
water	1.2 kilograms	5 cups + 1 tablespoon
sugar	100 grams	1/2 cup
ice cream stabilizer,	8 grams	3/4 teaspoon
such as Cremodan 30		
(see Sources, page 251)		
powdered milk	186 grams	1 1/2 cups
dextrose powder	50 grams	5 tablespoons
(see Sources, page 251)		+ 1/2 teaspoon
Trimoline *(invert sugar)*	50 grams	2 tablespoons
or corn syrup		
juice and zest of 2 lemons	--------	--------
olive oil	200 grams	15 tablespoons
For Finishing		
fresh eucalyptus leaves,	--------	--------
to form a bed		
extra-virgin olive oil,	--------	--------
for drizzling		
Maldon sea salt	--------	--------
fresh lemon zest	--------	--------
liquid nitrogen	--------	--------
or dry ice pellets		
(follow manufacturer's safety instructions; do not touch or consume)		

COCONUT, LIME, & PINEAPPLE

MAKES 12 SERVINGS

This coconut pudding with spiced pineapple is full of flavor and contrasting textures. It's also a great dessert option for anyone who's avoiding dairy or gluten.

INGREDIENT	WEIGHT	VOLUME
Coconut Pudding		
water, or more as needed	1 kilogram	1 liter or 4 1/4 cups
tapioca pearls	250 grams	1 2/3 cups
2 (14-ounce) cans coconut milk	--------	--------
coconut purée, preferably Perfect Purée brand (see Sources, page 250)	440 grams	1 3/4 cups
sugar	100 grams	1/2 cup
juice and zest of 2 limes	-------	--------
salt to taste	--------	--------

In a pot, bring the water to a boil, stir in the tapioca pearls, and continue cooking and stirring for about 15 minutes until the white pearls become transparent. You may need to add more water along the way.

Strain the tapioca, rinse lightly with cold water, then return to the pan along with the coconut milk, coconut purée, and sugar.

Cook the pudding over low heat for 5 to 10 minutes until it has thickened slightly and is creamy.

Remove the pudding from the heat and let cool, then stir in the lime juice and zest and salt to taste. The consistency should be similar to set yogurt. Place in the refrigerator until serving time; it will become a bit more firm. Gently reheat the pudding in a saucepan to loosen and warm it before serving. Serve at room temperature.

INGREDIENT	WEIGHT	VOLUME
Spiced Pineapple		
simple syrup	510 grams	2 cups +
(1:1 ratio of sugar to water)		2 tablespoons
1 star anise	--------	--------
coriander seeds	--------	1 tablespoon
red chili flakes	--------	2 teaspoons
1 pineapple, cut into 1/3-inch (1-cm) cubes	--------	--------

In a small pot, bring the simple syrup, star anise, coriander, and red chili flakes to a boil. Remove from the heat and allow to cool.

Put the prepared pineapple in a bowl and pour the spiced syrup over it. Allow the pineapple cubes to infuse for at least 2 to 3 hours, at room temperature.

Serve the coconut pudding at room temperature, topped with the spicy pineapple.

BOOZY
BEARS

MAKES 25 TO 30 SWEETS

I hate gimmicky food, but I love food when it's fun. These drunken homemade gummy bears are the ultimate adult sweet. You will need a gummy bear mold with 25 to 30 cavities (see Sources, page 251). I used whiskey here, but the possibilities are endless—feel free to experiment. Different alcohol contents and sugar levels might mean you have to adjust the recipe a bit, but don't let that stop you.

In a small saucepan, gently heat 130 grams of the whiskey with the powdered gelatin, stirring until the gelatin has dissolved.

In another small saucepan, heat the remaining 70 grams of whiskey with the sugar and glucose until the mixture registers 255°F on a Thermapen.

Cool the syrup to 212°F, pour it over the gelatin mixture, and mix well. Pour into the gummy bear molds and let set in the fridge for at least 1 hour, or until firm.

Remove the mold and enjoy.

INGREDIENT	WEIGHT	VOLUME
whiskey	200 grams	14 tablespoons
powdered gelatin	15 grams	4 3/4 teaspoons
sugar	50 grams	1/4 cup
glucose or corn syrup	200 grams	9 1/2 tablespoons
(see Sources, page 251)		

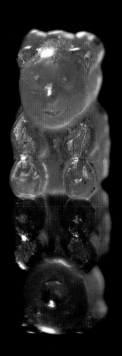
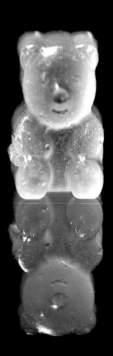

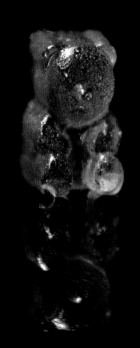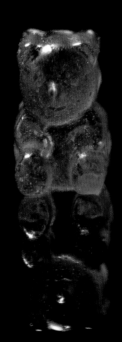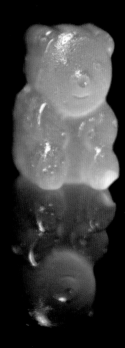

ACKNOWLEDGMENTS

Massive thanks to Daniel Melamud at Rizzoli for giving me the opportunity to write this book. Thank you for believing in me and for the constant support.

Additional thanks to Geoffrey Dunne, who designed the book and made it look so great.

For Jade Young, who has pretty much taken every photo of food I have ever done and always made it look perfect, many thanks for the years of support; I feel very honored to be able to work with such talent.

To Ivan Halpern for the process shots and support, as well as Michelle Chen and Michael Brathwaite, for their help with all the photo shoots.

And to all the chefs I have worked with past and present, Thank you.

IN DEDICATION

This book is dedicated to my amazingly beautiful wife, Kerry, who picked me up every time I fell and never let me give up on this demanding industry;

and to my baby daughter, Matilda, and our newest edition, Archibald, who both taught me that if I smile at the world, the world will smile back. You inspire me, each and every day.

IN MEMORY

This book was created in memory of

my mother, Marilyn,
my father, Malcolm,
my granny, Irene,
and my father-in-law, Andy.

I owe everything to all of you for different reasons. You all taught me to never give up on a dream and supported me unequivocally throughout. I hope you're looking down and smiling.

SOURCES

BUTTER	Isigny Sainte-Mère lightly salted butter available at amazon.com
	Black truffle butter available at dartagnan.com/home
CHEESE	Cabot clothbound aged cheddar available at murrayscheese.com
	Fromage d'Affinois cheese with black truffle available at murrayscheese.com
CHOCOLATE & COCOA BUTTER	Valrhona chocolate products including gianduja available at valrhona-chocolate.com/baking-products.html
	Extra Brute cocoa powder available at jet.com
	Cocoa butter pistoles available at amazon.com
CONFIT	Duck confit available at dartagnan.com/home
DISTILLED WATER	Distilled water available at most large pharmacies
FLAVORINGS	Madagascar vanilla beans available at amazon.com
	Monin rose syrup available at amazon.com
	Crème de banane available at most liquor stores
	Citric acid available at amazon.com
FLOUR	King Arthur flours available at most large grocery stores and at kingarthurflour.com
FOOD COLORING	Food coloring gel and powders as well as gold leaves available at auifinefoods.com and amazon.com
FRUIT-BASED PRODUCTS	Fruit purées from Boiron available at amazon.com
	Blood orange concentrate available at perfectpuree.com
	Yuzu juice available at most Asian supermarkets
	Freeze-dried raspberries available at amazon.com
GLAZES	Mirror glaze available at valrhona-chocolate.com/baking-products.com
	Neutral glaze available at amazon.com

PACKAGING	Cellophane wrappers available at clearcellobags.com
PURÉES AND PASTES	Fruit purées from Boiron available at amazon.com
	Sweetened and pure roasted pistachio paste from Sevarome available at amazon.com
	Black sesame paste from Marumoto Jun Neri available at amazon.com
	White miso available at most Asian supermarkets
SALT, PEPPER, AND AROMATICS	Maldon sea salt available at most large grocery stores or specialty stores
	Smoked black pepper available at amazon.com
SETTING AGENTS	Pectin available at amazon.com
	Silver gelatin sheets and powdered gelatin available at amazon.com
SILICONE MOLDS & BAKING LINERS	Silicone molds and pan liners available at jbprince.com
STABILIZERS	Cremodan 30 available at amazon.com
	Cremodan 64 available at amazon.com
SWEETENERS	Dextrose powder available at amazon.com
	Glucose syrup available at amazon.com
	Golden syrup available at amazon.com
	Pearl sugar available at amazon.com
THICKENERS	Sodium alginate available at amazon.com
	Calcium lactate gluconate available at amazon.com
TRUFFLES	Black truffle shavings available at dartagnan.com/home
YEAST	SAF Instant Yeast, gold label, available at amazon.com
	Fresh yeast available at amazon.com

INDEX

First published in the United States of America in 2019 by
Rizzoli International Publications, Inc.
300 Park Avenue South
New York, NY 10010
www.rizzoliusa.com

Text © 2019 Rory Macdonald
Photographs © 2019 Jade Young

Editor: Daniel Melamud
Design: Geoffrey Dunne
Copyediting: Sarah Scheffel
Proofreading: Liana Krissoff
Production: Colin Hough Trapp

ISBN-13: 978-0-8478-6384-6
Library of Congress Control Number: 2018960490

2019 2020 2021 2022 / 10 9 8 7 6 5 4 3 2 1
Printed in China